INDIAN CUISINE
Vegetarian

INDIAN * CUISINE

* Vegetarian *

Tiger Books International

London

Acknowledgement:

*Grateful thanks to Madhu Arora, Kiran Kapoor and Mili Paul
for having tried, tested and making available
the dishes for photography.*

This edition published in 1996 by:
Tiger Books International PLC, Twickenham

ISBN: 1-85501-813-6

Project Coordinator:
Arti Arora

Production:
N.K. Nigam, Gautam Dey, Abhijeet Raha

Conceived & Designed by
Pramod Kapoor
at
Roli Books CAD Centre

Photographer
Dheeraj Paul

Other photographs by:
Hemant Mehta: Cover and page 58
Neeraj Paul: 14, 24, 26, 36, 38, 46, 49, 54, 56, 76, 80

Printed and bound by:
Star Standard Industries Pte. Ltd., Singapore

CONTENTS

———— ✳ ————

7

To get you acquainted...

9

Spices—The Sweet & Sour of Indian Food

10

Basic Indian Recipes

11

Snacks and Starters

29

Tandoori and Dry Dishes

41

Stir-fried Dishes

49

Curry Dishes

65

Accompaniments and Desserts

84

Index

Kadhai (Wok)

Belan (Rolling pin) - **Chakla** (Flour board)

Tawa (Griddle)

Chimta (Tongs)

Kaddoo kas (Grater)

Masaaldaan (Spice container)

Hamam dasta (Mortar pestle)

Handi (Heavy-bottomed pot)

Karchi (Ladles)

Pateela (Deep pot)

TO GET YOU ACQUAINTED........

The main stable of the dining table in India is its extensive repertoire of vegetarian dishes. With millions of diners having perfected the cuisine over generations, it is hardly surprising that vegetarian cooking in India is not a grim exercise in dining, but a rich exploration of the variety of Indian cuisine.

Seasonal vegetables - like Punjab's *sarson ka saag* (curried Mustard greens) with *makki ki roti* (Indian maize bread) for example - inspire cooking. *Paneer* (cottage cheese) and mushrooms are vegetarian ingredients used for party foods as a replacement for meats, and home food generally tends to be lighter than party food, though the method of cooking might be almost similar.

Indian cuisine has a range and variety that is extraordinary, with each region contributing its own flavour. Modern Indian cooking borrows selectively from these diverse styles, assimilates and adapts them to suit the palate. The richness of Indian food, therefore continues to grow.

Regional differences in food are often so great that they make for entirely different cuisines. What is common are the raw ingredients, the vegetables and meats, and the spices. But, while the greater part of India is vegetarian, there are other regions where meat and chicken are considered an essential part of the daily meal. In Bengal, fish is an obsession and is referred to as *jal toru*, an underwater vegetable.

Indian food is usually eaten without starters, soups or courses, though in restaurants it is presented in this manner for less familiar diners. The main meal is eaten with either rice or *roti*, and includes at least one lentil curry called *daal*, a selection of vegetarian servings, a meat, chicken or fish fry, a sampling of chutneys and pickles, and *dahi* (yoghurt). *Papad* is served with meals that may be sometimes accompanied by *lassi* (buttermilk) - which helps to induce sleep on a warm afternoon!. Desserts are not standard. Sweets, of course, are served with almost any Indian meal, and may take the form of a South Indian *halwa*, a delicate Lucknavi *kheer* or light Bengali sweets. But, depending on the region, these may be served after, during or before an Indian meal. No wonder Indian food continues to surprise - its serving and style almost as variable as its thousands of recipes.

Tej patta (Bay leaves)

Methi dana (Fenugreek seed)

Khus khus (Poppy seeds)

Ajwain (Carom seeds)

Javitri (Mace)

Raee (Mustard seeds)

Haldi (Turmeric powder)

Choti elaichi (Green cardamom)

Heeng (Asafoetida)

Laung (Cloves)

Bari elaichi (Black cardamom)

Amchur (Green mango powder)

Laal mirch (Red chilli)

Dhania (Coriander) *powder*

Kaali mirch (Black peppercorn)

SPICES — THE SWEET & SOUR OF INDIAN FOOD

The secret of Indian cuisine lies in its spices. Used lightly but in exciting combinations, they can leave the palate tingling for more, without actually taking a toll on one's digestion.

As the story goes, the West had discovered and traded with pockets of the Indian subcontinent, primarily for its rich spices.

Although, the beneficial uses of spices have been recorded in ancient treatises, but the usage has known to vary from region to region. Apart from making food palatable, spices also have inherent 'cooling' and 'warming' properties. They are added to the foods intended for pregnant women, for invalids, for the old and of course for the very young, to aid recovery or to impart stamina.

The basic Indian spices alongwith salt, are *jeera* (**cumin**) to impart fragrance to food, *haldi* (*turmeric*) to give colour, *laal mirch* (**red chilli**) to spice up the food. *Amchur* (*dry green mango powder*) adds piquancy and a mere pinch of *heeng* (**asafoetida**) adds a unique taste and also aids digestion. Fresh **coriander** is the most common garnish and also adds a light fragrance.

Since fruits are seen as energy-giving, **dried fruits** are used extensively in India. Parts of fruits, berries or vegetables are dried and stored, as condiments. Several seeds too are used, each with a marked taste.

Saunf (**fennel**) is added to desserts and some vegetarian dishes to act as a flavouring agent. *Methidana* (**fenugreek seeds**) give a touch of bitterness, *kalonji* (**black onion seeds**) is used in 'heavier' cooking or for pickles. *Raee* (**mustard seeds**) add sourness to food while *khus-khus* (**poppy seeds**) enhances the flavour of meat. Fresh *imli* (**tamarind**) imparts a sour taste and *kesar* (**saffron**), India's most expensive herb, imparts a fine fragrance alongwith a rich yellow colour.

That Indian spices can be used almost in any fashion and to enhance any taste, is obvious from the fact that Indian tea too uses spices!! *Elaichi* (**cardamom**) is added to tea for flavouring, while saffron and almonds are added to *kahwa* (Kashmiri tea).

Coconut chutney

Garam Masala

Ginger-garlic paste

Green chilli paste

BASIC INDIAN RECIPES

Coconut chutney: Grated **coconut** (160 gms), roasted **gram** (15 gms), **curry leaves** (8), **green chillies,** chopped (5), **ginger,** chopped (15 gms), **lentils (urad daal),** (5 gms), **mustard seeds** (5 gms), **oil** (15 ml) and **salt** (to taste). Grind coconut, green chillies, ginger and gram to a paste. Sauté mustard seeds, lentils and curry leaves. Stir in the ground paste, cook for 3-5 minutes. Allow to cool, refrigerate and use when required.

Garam masala (for 445 gms): Finely grind the following ingredients and store: **cumin seeds** (90 gms), **black pepper corns** (70 gms), **black cardamom seeds** (75 gms), **fennel seeds** (30 gms), **green cardamoms** (40 gms), **coriander seeds** (30 gms), **cloves** (20 gms), **cinnamon sticks** (20 x 2.5 cm), **mace powder** (20 gms), **black cumin seeds** (20 gms), **dry rose petals** (15 gms), **bay leaves** (15 gms), **ginger powder** (15 gms).

Ginger paste or **Garlic paste:** Soak **ginger / garlic cloves** (300 gms) overnight to soften the skin. Peel and chop roughly. Process until pulped. The pulp can be stored in an airtight container and refrigerated for 4-6 weeks.

Green Chilli paste: Take required quantity of **green chillies**, chop roughly and process until pulped.

Khoya: Boil **milk** (2 lts) in a *kadhai* (wok). Simmer till quantity is reduced to half, stirring occasionally. Continue cooking, now stirring constantly and scraping from the sides, till a thick paste-like consistency is obtained (1-1½ hrs.). Allow to cool.

Mint Chutney: Mint leaves (60 gms), **coriander leaves** (120 gms), **cumin seeds** (5 gms), **garlic cloves** (2), **green chilli** (1), **raw mango** (30 gms), **tomatoes** (45 gms), **salt** (to taste). Chop all ingredients, blend until paste-like. Refrigerate in an airtight container.

Onion paste: Peel and chop the **onions** (500 gms) in quarters. Process until pulped. Refrigerate in an airtight container for 4-6 weeks. For **Browned Onion Paste**, slice and fry the onions in a little oil, allow to cool before processing.

Paneer (Cottage Cheese): In a pot, put **milk** (3 lts) to boil. Just before it boils, add (90 ml/6 tbs) **lemon juice / vinegar** to curdle the milk. Strain the curdled milk through a muslin cloth, to allow all whey and moisture to drain. Still wrapped in the muslin, place **paneer** under a weight for 2-3 hours to allow to set into a block which can be cut or grated.

Khoy

Mint Chu

Onio past

Pan

SNACKS & STARTERS

Khandvi & Bedvi (recipe on following page) ▶

Khandvi

Serves: 4   Preparation time: 45 minutes   Cooking time: 7-10 minutes

Ingredients:

Gramflour (*besan*), sieved *250 gms / 1¼ cups*
Yoghurt, whisked .... *500 gms / 2½ cups*
Lemons *2*
Green chilli paste (page 10) .... *5 gms / 1 tsp*
Ginger paste (page 10) .... *8 gms / 1½ tsp*
Salt .... *15 gms / 1 tbs*
Turmeric(*haldi*) powder .... *a pinch*

Water .... *500 ml / 2½ cups*
Oil .... *20 ml / 4 tsp*
Mustard (*raee*) seeds .... *20 gms / 4 tsp*
Cucumber, chopped ....*70 gms / 4²/₃ tbs*
Capsicum, chopped ....*40 gms / 2²/₃ tbs*
Green coriander, chopped .... *20 gms / 4 tsp*
Coconut, grated .... *100 gms / ½ cup*

Method:

1. To the yoghurt, add juice of 2 lemons, green chilli paste, ginger paste, salt, turmeric powder and gramflour, whisk well to break all lumps. Mix in water and whisk again.

2. Cook the mixture till it is of quite thick consistency, stirring continuously to prevent it from sticking to the bottom.

3. Oil a smooth surface, pour the mixture and spread evenly to a thickness of 1 mm. Leave it to cool.

4. Heat oil, sauté mustard seeds till they crackle. Add cucumber, capsicum, coriander and coconut. Toss for a while till vegetables and coconut are cooked but still slightly crunchy. Sprinkle this over the cooked gramflour sheet.

5. Cut the sheet into 1½" strips. Roll each strip tightly, place on a platter and serve hot, garnished with chopped coriander and accompanied by Mint chutney (page 10).

Bedvi

Serves: 4   Preparation time: 55 minutes   Cooking time: 10 minutes

Ingredients:

Semolina (*suji*) ....*200 gms / 1 cup*
Flour, sieved ....*100 gms / ½ cup*
Salt .... *7 gms / 1½ tsp*
Water ....*145 ml / ¾ cup*
Lentils (*urad daal*), washed *100 gms / ½ cup*
Ginger, chopped .... *15 gms / 1 tbs*

Green chillies, chopped .... *10 gms / 2 tsp*
Onion (*kalonji*) seeds .... *a pinch*
Asafoetida (*heeng*) powder .... *a pinch*
Garam masala (page 10) .... *a pinch*
Vegetable soda ....*2½ gms / ½ tsp*
Oil .... *20 ml / 4 tsp + for frying*

◀ *Picture on preceding page*

Method:

1. Pick, wash and soak the lentils in water for 45 minutes.
2. Mix the flour, salt and semolina together. Add water and make a medium strong dough. Roughly flatten the dough with wet finger tips and divide into 16 equal parts.
3. **For the filling,** grind the drained lentils, ginger and green chillies to a paste. Add onion seeds, asafoetida, garam masala and soda powder. Divide into 16 equal parts.
4. Flatten one part of dough and place one part of the filling in it. Shape into a ball.
5. Roll out each ball to a diameter of 5 cm, using oil to avoid from sticking.
6. Deep fry in hot oil till golden brown. Drain excess oil and serve hot.

Sesame Seed coated Cheese Kababs

Serves: 4   Preparation time: 30 minutes   Cooking time: 15 minutes

Ingredients

Cottage cheese (*paneer*),
finely grated .... *500 gms*
Cardamom(*elaichi*) powder ..... *2 gms / ½ tsp*
Garam masala (page 10) .... *10 gms / 2 tsp*
Green chillies, chopped .... *5 gms / 1 tsp*
Green coriander, chopped .... *10 gms / 2 tsp*
Mace (*javitri*) powder .... *2 gms / ½ tsp*
Salt to taste

Onions, finely chopped .... *100 gms / ½ cup*
White pepper powder .... *5 gms / 1 tsp*
Yellow or Red chilli powder .... *6 gms / 1⅓ tsp*
Yoghurt, drained .... *400 gms / 2 cups*
Gramflour(*besan*)/Cornflour .. *50 gms / ¼ cup*
Sesame (*til*) seeds .... *100 gms / ½ cup*
Egg white (optional) *1*
Oil .... *100 ml / ½ cup*

Method:

* For Recipe of *paneer*, turn to page 10.

1. Combine all ingredients except gramflour/cornflour. Mix with wooden spoon and season to taste. Now add the gramflour/cornflour and mix for 2 minutes.
2. Divide the mixture into 20 equal balls. Compress each ball slightly to get a 4 cm round patty. Refrigerate the patties for 20 minutes.
3. Sprinkle with sesame seeds and shallow fry until crisp and golden in colour.
4. Alternatively, you could lightly coat each patty with beaten egg white, before sprinkling with sesame seeds and frying.
5. Serve hot, garnished with cucumber, tomato and onion slices and accompanied by Mint chutney (page 10).

Yam Kabab

Serves: 4   Preparation time: 20 minutes   Cooking time: 20 minutes

Ingredients:

Yam (*jimikand*) .... 1½ kg
Green chillies, finely chopped .. *4 gms / ¾ tsp*
Ginger, finely chopped .... *4 gms / ¾ tsp*
Salt .... *8 gms / 1½ tsp*
White pepper .... *4 gms / ¾ tsp*

Red chilli powder .... *4 gms / ¾ tsp*
Chaat masala .... *4 gms / ¾ tsp*
Green coriander, finely chopped *4gms /¾ tsp*
Bread crumbs .... *100 gms / ½ cup*
Oil .... *150 ml / ¾ cup*

Method:

1. Peel and wash the yam. Immerse in boiling water and cook until it becomes tender.

2. Remove from water, grate finely and squeeze out all excess water.

3. To the grated yam, add the remaining ingredients. Mix well and divide into 8 equal portions. Shape the portions into medallions.

4. Shallow fry each, on medium heat, till they become crisp and golden brown on both sides.

5. Serve hot, accompanied by Mint chutney (page 10).

Lentil Kabab

Serves: 4   Preparation time: 15 minutes   Cooking time: 25 minutes

Ingredients:

Lentils
(*malka masoor daal*) .... *300 gms / 1½ cups*
Water as required
Green chilli, deseeded, chopped *5 gms / 1 tsp*
Green coriander, chopped .... *10 gms / 2 tsp*
Ginger, finely chopped .... *10 gms / 2 tsp*
Salt to taste

Red chilli powder .... *a pinch*
Chaat masala .... *4 gms / ¾ tsp*
Bread crumbs (white) .... *50 gms / 3²/₃ tbs*
Cornflour .... *5 gms / 1 tsp*
Garam masala (page 10) .... *a pinch*
Oil for frying

Method:

1. Pick and wash the lentils, boil in water till they become soft. Drain and mash the lentils.

2. Add green chillies, coriander, ginger, salt, red chilli powder, chaat masala, bread crumbs, corn flour and garam masala. Mix well, divide and shape into 16 medallions.

3. Deep fry in hot oil until light brown in colour. Drain excess oil and serve hot.

◀ *Yam Kabab*

Assorted Fritters

Serves: 6   Preparation time: 10 minutes   Cooking time: 30 minutes

Ingredients:

Gramflour (*besan*),
sifted ....*135 gms / 3/4 cup*
Clarified butter (*ghee*)/Oil
+ for frying .... *10 ml / 2 tsp*
Lemon juice .... *15 ml / 1 tbs*
Cayenne pepper .... *a pinch*
Turmeric(*haldi*) powder .... *a pinch*
Garam masala (page 10) .... *5 gms / 1 tsp*
Coriander powder .... *10 gms / 2 tsp*
Salt.. *5 gms / 1 tsp*
Water, cold .... *135 ml / 3/5 cup*

Baking powder (optional) .... *3 gms / ½ tsp*
Fritter suggestions:
Potatoes—cut into rounds
Cauliflower flowerets
Spinach—medium sized leaves
Green chillies—medium sized, slit
lengthwise and filled with chaat masala
Cottage cheese (*paneer*)—cut into 2" x 4"
slices with chaat masala layered between 2
slices

Method:

    * For recipe of *paneer* turn to page 10

1. Combine together, the gramflour, clarified butter, lemon juice, cayenne pepper, turmeric powder, garam masala, ground coriander and salt. Mix well and add water (5 tbs). Whisk well to make batter lump-free. Slowly mix in more water till the consistency of batter resembles heavy cream and easily coats on the spoon.

2. Whisk again for about 3-5 minutes to further lighten the batter. Stir in baking powder if a cake-like crust is preferred.

3. Heat oil in a *kadhai* (wok) to upto 180 °C (335 °F). To check if oil is of right temperature, slip in a small spoonful of batter into the oil, if it rises and cooks immediately, the oil is ready.

4. Dip vegetables in the batter and slip one by one into the hot oil. Do not allow the fritters to stick to each other. Deep fry till the fritters are crisp and golden brown on each side.

5. Similarly, dip the cottage cheese sandwhich (with chaat masala filling) and the stuffed green chillies to coat evenly with the batter. Fry in the hot oil till crisp and golden brown on each side.

6. Serve hot, accompanied by Mint chutney (page 10) and /or Tomato Ketchup.

Mattar Kachori

Serves: 18   Preparation time: 1¼ hours   Cooking time: 1 hour

Ingredients:

Flour, levelled .... *400 gms / 2 cups*	Ginger, finely chopped .... *7 gms / 1½ tsp*
Salt .... *5 gms / 1 tsp*	Asafoetida (*heeng*) powder .... *a pinch*
Sugar .... *7 gms / 1½ tsp*	Garam masala (page 10) .... *5 gms / 1 tsp*
Clarified butter (*ghee*), ... *75 ml / 5 tbs*	Lemon juice .... *7 ml / 1½ tsp*
Peas, boiled and mashed . *500 gms / 2½ cups*	Baking soda .... *a pinch*
Water, chilled .... *105 ml / 7 tbs*	Oil for frying
Green chillies, deseeded	
and finely chopped *2-3*	

Method:

1. Blend flour, salt and sugar (½ tsp) in a mixing bowl. Add clarified butter (4 tbs), rub it in with your fingertips until it is fully incorporated and the mixture resembles coarse bread crumbs. Mix in mashed peas (½ cup). Add ice water and knead to form a smooth and pliable dough. Cover with plastic wrap and set aside for ½-1 hour.

2. **For the filling,** heat clarified butter (1 tbs) in a pan, add green chillies, ginger and fry for ½ minute, mix in the asafoetida, peas (1½ cups), garam masala, lemon juice, baking soda and sugar (1 tsp). Stir fry for 1 minute. Remove and allow to cool. Divide the filling into 18 portions.

3. Divide the dough into 18 even portions. Shape each portion into a patty. Cover with a damp towel or plastic wrap and set aside.

4. Flatten each patty into a 2½" (6.5 cm) round. Place one portion of filling in the centre of the dough, then bring the sides of the dough over the filling to enclose completely. Pinch the seams together until thoroughly sealed. Cover with a plastic wrap or a moist towel. Keep aside. Shape and stuff the remaining pieces.

5. Heat oil in a *kadhai* (wok) upto 150 °C (300 °F). Slip in a few patties, (seam side down), at a time. Fry until pale golden in colour and until they sound hollow when tapped. The crust should be delicately blistered and crisp. Drain excess oil and serve hot, accompanied by Mint chutney (page 10) and / or Tomato Ketchup.

◀ *1.Mattar Kachori*

Khasta Kachori

Serves: 18   Preparation time: 1¼ hours   Cooking time: 1 hour

Ingredients:

Flour, levelled .... *300 gms / 1½ cups*
Wheatflour .... *100 gms / ½ cup*
Salt .... *8 gms / 1½ tsp*
Clarified butter (*ghee*), ... *90 ml / 6 tbs*
Water, chilled .... *105 ml / 7 tbs*
Lentils (*split moong daal*), without skin
(soaked for 3-5 hours) .... *100 gms / ½ cup*

Cumin (*jeera*), seeds .... *5 gms / 1 tsp*
Caraway seeds............................ *4 gms / ¾ tsp*
Fennel (*saunf*), seeds .... *8 gms / 1½ tsp*
Coriander seeds .... *23 gms / 1½ tbs*
Black pepper, coarsely ground .. *4 gms / ¾ tsp*
Water... *150 ml / 2/3 cup*
Oil for frying

Method:

1. Blend the flours and salt (1½ tsp) in a mixing bowl. Add clarified butter (4 tbs), rub it in with your fingertips until it is fully incorporated and the mixture resembles coarse bread crumbs. Add ice water and knead to form a smooth and pliable dough. Cover with plastic and set aside for ½-1 hour.

2. **For the filling**, drain the soaked lentils and grind coarsely. Heat clarified butter (2 tbs) in a pan, add cumin seeds, caraway seeds, fennel seeds and coriander seeds. Fry until they splutter. Stir in black pepper, water and the coarsely ground lentils. Bring to a boil, lower heat and simmer, partially covered until the water is absorbed and lentils have softened but are still slightly firm. Allow to cool, mix in salt to taste and divide into 18 equal portions.

3. Divide the dough into 18 even portions. Shape each portion into a patty. Cover with a damp towel or plastic wrap and set aside.

4. Flatten each patty into a 2½" (6.5 cm) round. Place one portion of filling in the centre of the dough, then bring the sides of the dough over the filling, to enclose completely. Pinch the seams together until thoroughly sealed. Cover with a plastic wrap or a moist towel. Keep aside. Shape and stuff the remaining pieces.

5. Heat oil in a *kadhai* (wok) upto 150 °C (300 °F). Slip in a few patties, (seam side down), at a time. Fry until pale golden in colour and until they sound hollow when tapped. The crust should be delicately blistered and crisp. Drain excess oil and serve hot, accompanied by

◀ *2. Khasta Kachori; 3. Aloo Kachori (picture on page 18)*

Aloo Kachori

Serves: 18　　　　　Preparation time: 1¼ hours　　　　　Cooking time: 1 hour

Ingredients:

Flour, levelled .... *400 gms / 2 cups*	Cumin (*jeera*), ground .... *5 gms / 1 tsp*
Salt .... *5 gms / 1 tsp*	Fennel (*saunf*), ground .... *2 gms / ½ tsp*
Clarified butter (*ghee*), ... *60 ml / 4 tbs*	Garam masala (page 10) .... *5 gms / 1 tsp*
Yoghurt .... *30 ml / 2 tbs*	Turmeric(*haldi*) powder .... *a pinch*
Water, chilled .... *105 ml / 7 tbs*	Lemon juice .... *15 ml / 1 tbs*
Green chillies, deseeded, finely chopped *2-3*	Salt .... *5 gms / 1 tsp*
Ginger, finely chopped .... *7 gms / 1½ tsp*	Green coriander / Parsley,
Potatoes, boiled and	finely chopped .... *30 gms / 2 tbs*
mashed .... *300 gms / 1½ cups*	Oil for frying
Coriander powder .... *7 gms / 1½ tsp*	

Method:

1. Blend flour and salt in a mixing bowl. Add clarified butter (*ghee*), rub it in with your fingertips until it is fully incorporated and the mixture resembles coarse bread crumbs. Add yoghurt, ice water (6 tbs) and knead to make a smooth and pliable dough. Cover with plastic wrap and set aside for ½-1 hour.

2. **For the filling**, combine the remaining ingredients in a mixing bowl and knead with your hands until well blended. Divide into 18 portions, keep aside.

3. Divide the dough into 18 even portions. Shape each portion into a patty. Cover with a damp towel or plastic wrap and set aside.

4. Flatten each patty into a 2½" (6.5 cm) round. Place one portion of filling in the centre of the dough, then bring the sides of the dough over the filling, to enclose completely. Pinch the seams together until thoroughly sealed. Cover with a plastic wrap or a moist towel. Keep aside. Shape and stuff the remaining pieces.

5. Heat oil in a *kadhai* (wok) upto 150 °C (300 °F). Slip in a few patties (seam side down), at a time. Fry until pale golden in colour and until they sound hollow when tapped. The crust should be delicately blistered and crisp. Drain excess oil and serve hot, accompanied by Mint chutney (page 10) and / or Tomato Ketchup.

Batter coated stuffed Tomatoes

Serves: 6   Preparation time: 30-40 minutes   Cooking time: 30-40 minutes

Ingredients:

Tomatoes .... *340-455 gms*	**For the batter:**
Cottage cheese (*paneer*) ... *140 gms / 3/5 cup*	Gramflour (*besan*), sifted .... *60 gms / 4 tbs*
Black pepper, ground .... *1 gm / ¼ tsp*	Cayenne pepper .... *1 gm / ¼ tsp*
Asafoetida (*heeng*) powder .... *1 gm / ¼ tsp*	Salt .... *1 gm / ¼ tsp*
Green coriander, chopped .... *30 gms / 2 tbs*	Baking powder .... *1 gm / ¼ tsp*
Oil for frying	Water, cold .... *50 ml / ¼ cup*

Method:

1. Slice stems off the tomatoes, hollow out centres, drain upside down on a paper towel.
2. Knead cottage cheese and spices together. Fill each tomato cup with the mixture.
3. Mix the ingredients for the batter, adding water slowly. Whisk until batter is smooth and thick enough to seal in the filling and to evenly coat the tomatoes.
4. Dip each filled tomato in batter, coating evenly. Deep fry until golden brown on all sides. Remove, drain on paper towels. Serve hot.

Tandoori Potatoes

Serves: 4   Preparation time: 20 minutes   Cooking time: 15 minutes

Ingredients:

Potatoes (large), peeled .... *1 kg*	Cashewnuts, chopped .... *15 gms / 1 tbs*
Oil for frying	Raisins .... *10 gms / 2 tsp*
Salt to taste	Clarified butter (*ghee*) .... *10 ml / 2 tsp*
Red chilli powder .... *5 gms / 1 tsp*	Cottage cheese (*paneer*),
Garammasala (page 10) .... *a pinch*	grated .... *20 gms / 4 tsp*
Lemon juice .... *5 ml / 1 tsp*	Chaat masala .... *2½ gms / ½ tsp*

Method:

* For recipe of *paneer*, turn to page 10.

1. Scoop out the centres of the potatoes. Deep fry shells and centres separately till the sides become crisp. Allow centres to cool and mash.
2. Mix together mashed potatoes, salt, red chilli, garam masala, lemon juice, cashewnuts, raisins and clarified butter. Fill the potato cases with this and top up with cottage cheese.
3. Skewer 4 pieces each, per skewer and grill till golden brown in colour.
4. Sprinkle chaat masala and serve hot, garnished with chopped coriander.

◀ *Batter coated stuffed Tomatoes*

Steamed Rice Flour Patty (*Idli*)

Serves: 4   Preparation time: 24 hours   Cooking time: 10 minutes

Ingredients

Parboiled rice ....*300 gms / 1½ cups*   Salt to taste
Lentils (*urad daal*), husked   *150 gms /¾ cup*   Oil to grease moulds

Method:

1. Wash and soak the rice for 6-7 hours, then grind to a coarse paste. Keep aside.
2. Soak lentils (1 hr), drain and blend with very little water to obtain a thick paste-like consistency. Mix the lentil paste, rice flour paste and salt, set aside to ferment (6 hrs).
3. Grease *idli* moulds, fill half-way with batter and steam for 8-10 minutes. A toothpick inserted in the *idli* should come out clean if it is cooked. (If no moulds are available then use small, heat proof bowls and steam in a double boiler.)
4. Demould *idlis,* place on individual plates, dot with hot lentil powder (optional), serve hot accompanied by Coconut chutney (page10) and *Sambhar* (below).

Lentil Curry (*Sambhar*)

Serves: 4   Preparation time:40 minutes   Cooking time:1 hour

Ingredients:

Lentils (*arhar daal*) ....*200 gms / 1 cup*
Tamarind (*imlee*) pulp ....*15 gms / 1 tbs*
Coconut, grated ....*75 gms / 5 tbs*
Coriander seeds ....*5 gms / 1 tsp*
Cumin (*jeera*) seeds ....*10 gms / 2 tsp*
Groundnut oil ....*45 ml / 3 tbs*
Red chillies, whole *2*
Mustard (*raee*) seeds ....*5 gms / 1 tsp*
Asafoetida (*heeng*) ....*a pinch*
Curry leaves *15*

Green chillies, slit *4*
Green drumsticks,
chopped roughly .... *200 gms*
Turmeric(*haldi*) powder .... *5 gms / 1 tsp*
Red chilli powder ....*5 gms / 1 tsp*
Onions, sliced ....*180 gms / ¾ cup*
Tomatoes, quartered ....*300 gms / 1¼ cups*
Salt to taste
Jaggery (soaked in 2 tbs water)   *10 gms / 2 tsp*
Green coriander, chopped .... *20 gms / 4 tsp*

Method:

1. Wash and soak lentils for 30 minutes.
2. Dissolve tamarind in water (1 cup).
3. Drain lentils and boil in a *handi* (pot) with water (3½ cups) till completely cooked.
4. Prepare *sambhar* paste, by lightly roasting grated coconut, coriander seeds, cumin and whole red chillies. Grind to a paste and keep aside.

◀ *Steamed Rice Flour Patty (Idli)*

5. Heat oil (2 tbs), sauté mustard seeds and asafoetida till the seeds crackle. Add curry leaves, green chillies, tamarind water, green drumsticks, turmeric, red chilli powder, onions, tomatoes and salt. Bring to a boil and simmer for 7-8 minutes.
6. Stir in the prepared paste, the cooked lentils and the dissolved jaggery. Bring to a boil and simmer for 8-10 minutes.
7. Sprinkle chopped coriander and serve hot, as an accompaniment to *Idli* (page 25), *Dosa* (below) or steamed rice.

Rice Flour Pancakes (*Dosa*)

Serves: 4   Preparation time: Overnight+6½ hour   Cooking time: 30 minutes

Ingredients:

For Pancakes (*dosa*)

Parboiled rice .... *225 gms*	Mustard (*raee*) seeds .... *5 gms / 1 tsp*
Lentils (*urad daal*), husked *150 gms / ¾ cup*	Bengal gram(*chana daal*), split *15 gms /1 tbs*
Fenugreek (*methi*) seeds .... *2½ gms / ½ tsp*	Onions, sliced .... *120 gms / ½ cup*
Oil ....*80 ml / 5 1/3 tbs*	Green chillies, chopped *4*
Water .... *45 ml / 3 tbs*	Turmeric(*haldi*) powder .... *5 gms / 1 tsp*
Salt to taste	Salt to taste
For Potato filling:	Lemon juice .... *15 ml / 1 tbs*
Potatoes, boiled and mashed *200 gms / 1 cup*	Curry leaves *10*
Oil .... *60 ml / 4 tbs*	Green coriander, chopped .... *20 gms / 4 tsp*

Method:

1. Soak the rice and lentils overnight alongwith fenugreek seeds. Blend with water (3 tbs) to make a fine paste. Keep aside and allow to ferment for 5-6 hours.
2. Heat oil in a *kadhai* (wok), sauté mustard seeds till they crackle, add gram, stir until light brown. Stir in onions, sauté until transparent. Mix in green chillies, turmeric, salt and lemon juice. Add potatoes, curry leaves and coriander. Cook for 5 minutes.
3. Heat a *tawa* (griddle). Season it by wiping the surface (once only) with ½ onion wrapped in muslin and dipped in oil. Reduce heat, thinly spread a ladleful of batter by moving the ladle in concentric circles. Cook for 2 minutes.
4. Loosen edges by dotting with oil. Flip over, semi-cook for a few seconds. Flip over again, place 2 tbs of potato mixture in the centre, dot with butter and fold both sides over. Serve hot, accompanied by Coconut chutney (page 10) and *Sambhar* (above).

◀ *Rice Flour Pancakes (Dosa)*

Cottage Cheese Kathi Kabab

Serves: 4   Preparation time: 30 minutes   Cooking time: 15 minutes

Ingredients:

Cottage cheese (*paneer*), 1" cubes *450 gms*
Poppy (*khus khus*) seeds ....*2½ gms / ½ tsp*
Coriander seeds .... *5 gms / 1 tsp*
Cloves (*laung*) *6*
Black cardamoms(*bari elaichi*) *4*
Cinnamon stick (*daalchini*) (1" piece) *1*
Black peppercorns *15*
Cumin (*jeera*) seeds .... *5 gms / 1 tsp*
Onions, chopped ....*80 gms / ⅓ cup*
Garlic cloves, chopped *10*
Ginger, chopped .... *15 gms / 1 tbs*

Yoghurt .... *100 gms / ½ cup*
Salt to taste
Red chilli powder .... *5 gms / 1 tsp*
Turmeric(*haldi*) powder .... *5 gms / 1 tsp*
Gram, roasted and powdered.. *15 gms / 1 tbs*
Salad oil .... *15 gms / 1 tbs*
Butter for brushing
Dry mango powder (*amchoor*) *5 gms / 1 tsp*
Garam masala(page 10) .... *5 gms / 1 tsp*
Lemon juice .... *15 ml / 1 tbs*
Paranthas (page 75) *4*

Method:

   * For recipe of *paneer,* turn to page 10.

1. Lightly broil poppy and coriander seeds, cloves, cardamoms, cinnamon, peppercorns and cumin.

2. Blend the spices alongwith the onion, garlic and ginger.

3. Whisk together, yoghurt, salt, red chilli powder, turmeric powder, gram flour and salad oil.

4. Coat cottage cheese cubes evenly with the prepared mixture.

5. Roast in a hot grill (163 °C / 325 °F) for 12-15 minutes, turning 2-3 times to roast evenly.

6. Brush with butter. Sprinkle mango powder, garam masala and lemon juice.

7. Divide into four portions, place each portion in the centre of one *parantha*. Roll each *parantha* tightly, wrapping one end in aluminium foil or butter paper.

8. Serve hot, accompanied by Mint chutney (page 10) and Onion salad.

TANDOORI & DRY

Crunchy Okra (recipe on following page) ▶

Crunchy Okra

Serves: 4-6   Preparation time: 40 minutes   Cooking time: 30 minutes

Ingredients:

Okra (*bhindi*) .... *500 gms*
Salt to taste
Red chilli powder .... *5 gms / 1 tsp*
Garam masala (page 10) .... *5 gms / 1 tsp*
Dry mango powder (*amchoor*) *3 gms / ½ tsp*

Chaat masala .... *3 gms / ½ tsp*
Gramflour (*besan*) .... *45 gms / 3 tbs*
Oil for frying
Ginger, julienned .... *7 gms / 1½ tsp*
Green chillies, sliced (optional) *2*

Method:

1. Snip off both ends of each okra, slice length-wise into four slices.
2. Spread all sliced okra on a flat dish and sprinkle evenly with salt, chilli powder, garam masala, mango powder and chaat masala. Mix gently to coat okra evenly.
3. Sprinkle gram flour over the okra and mix in so they are coated evenly, preferably without adding any water.
4. Divide the okra into two portions.
5. Heat oil in a *kadhai* (wok) or a pan till it is smoking.
6. Fry one portion coated okra slices, separating each lightly with a fork. Do not allow slices to stick to each other.
7. Remove from oil when both sides are crispy and brown in colour.
8. Similarly, fry the other portion.
9. Garnish with julienned ginger and green chillies.
10. Serve hot, accompanied by Chappatis (page 73).

◀ *Picture on preceding page*

Cauliflower Seasoned with Ginger

Serves: 4-5   Preparation time: 10 minutes   Cooking time: 25 minutes

Ingredients:

Cauliflower, cut into small flowerets .... *1 kg*
Oil .... *75 ml / 5 tbs*
Onions, finely chopped .... *150 gms / ¾ cup*
Ginger paste (page 10) .... *20 gms / 4 tsp*
Garlic paste (page 10) .... *20 gms / 4 tsp*
Turmeric(*haldi*) powder .... *10 gms / 2 tsp*
Red chilli powder .... *10 gms / 2 tsp*
White pepper powder .... *5 gms / 1 tsp*

Coriander powder .... *10 gms / 2 tsp*
Tomatoes, skinned and
chopped .... *100 gms / ½ cup*
Salt to taste
Garam masala (page 10) .... *10 gms / 2 tsp*
Butter .... *10 gms / 2 tsp*
Ginger, julienned .... *10 gms / 2 tsp*
Green coriander, chopped .... *10 gms / 2 tsp*

Method:

1. Wash the cauliflower thoroughly.

2. Heat oil in a pan. Add onions and sauté over medium heat.

3. Add ginger and garlic pastes, turmeric powder, red chilli powder, white pepper, coriander powder and tomatoes and sauté for 45-60 seconds.

4. Add the cauliflower, stir in water (100 ml / ½ cup). Cover and cook for 15 minutes till the liquid dries up.

5. Season with salt and garam masala.

6. In a separate pan, heat the butter. Add the julienned ginger and lightly sauté.

7. Sprinkle the sautéd ginger over the cauliflower.

8. Garnish with chopped coriander and serve hot, accompanied by Chappati (page 73) or Parantha (page 75).

Crispy Cauliflower

Serves: 4   Preparation: 15 minutes   Cooking: 15 minutes

Ingredients:

Cauliflower, 5 small whole ones .... *1 kg*
Salt to taste
Turmeric(*haldi*) powder .... *10 gms / 2 tsp*
Gramflour (*besan*) .... *200 gms/1 cup*
Carom (*ajwain*) seeds .... *6 gms / 1¹/₃ tsp*
Lemon juice ....*3 ml / ½ tsp*
Green coriander, finely chopped *20 gms / 4 tsp*

Green chillies, finely chopped   *20 gms / 4 tsp*
Yoghurt ....*100 gms / ½ cup*
Ginger paste (page 10) .... *10 gms / 2 tsp*
Garlic paste (page 10) .... *10 gms / 2 tsp*
Garam masala (page 10) ....*8 gms / 1²/₃ tsp*
Red or Yellow chilli powder ..... *10 gms / 2 tsp*
Oil ....*500 ml / 2½ cups*

Method:

1. Boil sufficient water to immerse the cauliflowers. Add salt (1 tsp) and turmeric powder.
2. Gradually add the cauliflowers to this brine solution. Cook for 8-10 minutes over medium heat until the cauliflowers are half cooked. Drain and keep aside.
3. Prepare a batter with the gramflour (*besan*), carom seeds, lemon juice, coriander, green chillies, yoghurt, ginger-garlic pastes, garam masala, chilli powder, salt and just enough water to have a thick and smooth consistency.
4. Heat oil in a *kadhai* (wok). Dip each cauliflower into the batter, coat evenly and deep fry over medium heat till golden in colour and crisp.
5. Serve hot, accompanied by Mint chutney (page 10).

Stuffed Capsicum

Serves: 4-5   Preparation time: 15 minutes   Cooking time: 1 hour

Ingredients:

Capsicums, (each 70 gms approx.) *10*
Oil .... *60 ml / 4 tbs*
Onions, chopped .... *100 gms / ½ cup*
Cashewnuts, chopped .... *20 gms / 4 tsp*
Raisins .... *20 gms / 4 tsp*
White pepper .... *5 gms / 1 tsp*
Garam masala (page 10) ....*8 gms / 1²/₃ tsp*
Green chillies, finely chopped   *10 gms / 2 tsp*

Ginger, finely chopped .... *10 gms / 2 tsp*
Green coriander, chopped .... 15 gms / 1 tbs
Salt to taste
Potatoes, boiled and mashed .... *750 gms*
Butter for basting .... *40 gms / 2²/₃ tbs*
For the Sauce:
Oil .... *25 ml / 5 tsp*
Green cardamoms(*choti elaichi*) *3 gms /²/₃ tsp*

◀ *Crispy Cauliflower*

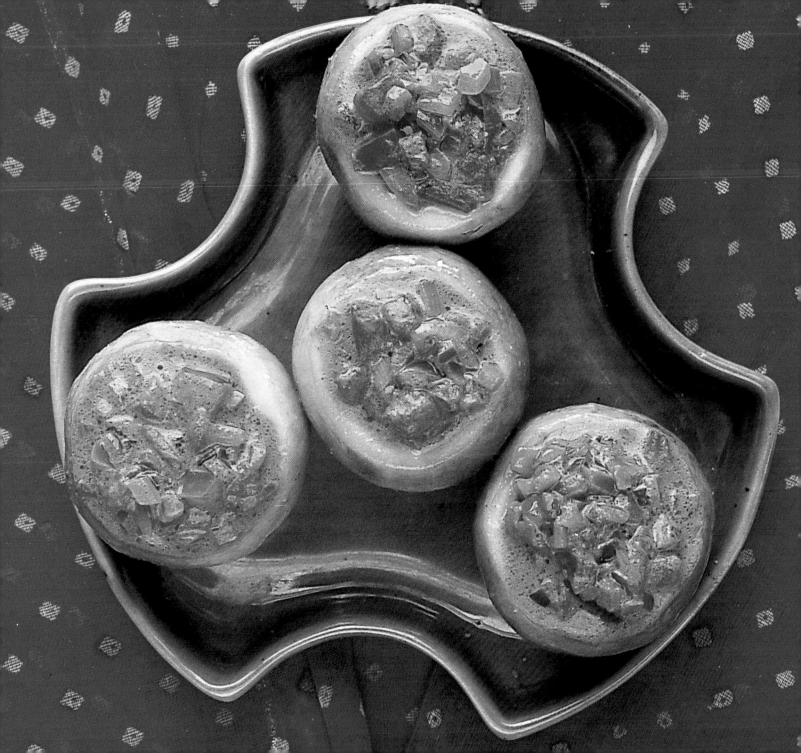

Bay leaf (*tej patta*) *1*	Mace (*javitri*) powder .... *3 gms /²/₃ tsp*
Onions, sliced .... *20 gms / 4 tsp*	Salt to taste
Garlic cloves (3) .... *10 gms*	Cream .... *60 ml / 4 tbs*
Tomatoes, chopped .... *300 gms / 1½ cups*	

Method:

1. Slice stem off the capsicum, remove seeds and keep aside.
2. Heat oil in a pan, sauté onions, cashewnuts and raisins over low heat for 5-6 min.
3. Add white pepper, garam masala, green chillies, ginger, half of the green coriander, salt and potatoes, stir for 5 minutes. Remove from heat.
4. Fill each capsicum with the potato mixture and arrange the capsicums in a greased baking dish. Bake at 175 °C (350 °F) for 15-20 minutes, basting with melted butter.
5. **For the sauce**, heat oil in a pan, sauté cardamoms, bay leaf, onions, garlic cloves and tomatoes. Add water (2 cups), cook for 20 minutes. Strain sauce through a fine sieve. Stir in the mace, salt and cream.
6. Remove capsicums from the oven, arrange them on a platter. Pour the sauce over the capsicums, sprinkle remaining green coriander and serve.

Stuffed Courgettes (*Teenda*)

Serves: 2-4   Preparation time:20 minutes   Cooking time:25 minutes

Ingredients:

Courgettes *(teenda)* *4*	Chilli powder .... *5 gms / 1 tsp*
Oil + for frying .... *60 gms / 4 tbs*	Dried mango powder (*amchoor*) ....
Onion, finely chopped *1*	.... *10 gms / 2 tsp*
Tomatoes, chopped *2*	Salt to taste
Garam masala (page 10) .... *15 gms / 1 tbs*	Cream .... *60 gms / 4 tbs*

Method:

1. Wash and dry the courgettes. Slice top to form a lid. Scoop out the center, keep aside.
2. Heat oil in a pan, deep fry the courgettes for 1-2 minutes from all sides. Drain excess oil and keep aside.
3. Heat oil (4 tbs) in a pan, sauté onion until transparent. Mix in tomatoes, cook for 4-5 minutes, add garam masala, chilli powder, mango powder and salt. Stir in the cream. Cover and cook on low heat for a few minutes.
4. Fill each courgette cup with onion-tomato mixture, replace lid, place on a baking tray and bake in a preheated oven (175 °C/350 °F) for 5-7 min. Remove lid and serve hot.

◀ *Stuffed Courgettes (Teenda)*

Cottage Cheese Tikka

Serves: 4-5   Preparation time: 2¼ hours   Cooking time: 10 minutes

Ingredients:

Cottage cheese (*paneer*) .... *1 kg*
Black cumin (*shah jeera*) .... *3 gms /1 ½ tsp*
White pepper .... *5 gms / 1 tsp*
Garam masala (page 10) .... *10 gms / 2 tsp*
Turmeric(*haldi*) powder .... *5 gms / 1 tsp*
Lemon juice .... *25 ml / 5 tsp*
Salt to taste
Cream .... *150 ml / ¾ cup*
Yoghurt, drained .... *150 gms / ¾ cup*

Gramflour (*besan*)/Cornflour ... *30 gms / 2 tbs*
Red chilli powder .... *10 gms / 2 tsp*
Saffron .... *3 gms / ½ tsp*
Ginger paste (page 10) .... *15 gms / 1 tbs*
Garlic paste (page 10) .... *15 gms / 1 tbs*
Fenugreek (*kasoori methi*) powder
.... *5 gms / 1 tsp*
Butter to baste
Chaat masala .... *10 gms / 2 tsp*

Method:

* For recipe of *paneer,* turn to page 10.

1. Wash and cut the cottage cheese into 2" cubes (30 pieces).

2. Mix the black cumin, white pepper, garam masala, turmeric powder, two-thirds of the lemon juice and salt. Sprinkle over the cottage cheese cubes. Refrigerate for 1 hour.

3. Mix cream, yoghurt and gramflour/cornflour in a bowl, add the remaining ingredients (except butter) and whisk well to make a smooth batter.

4. Add the cottage cheese cubes to this, coat evenly and leave to marinate for at least 1 hour.

5. Preheat the oven to 150-75 °C (300-50 °F).

6. Thread the cottage cheese cubes onto a skewer, 2 cm apart.

7. Roast in an oven/tandoor/charcoal grill for 5-6 minutes, basting occasionally with melted butter.

8. Sprinkle chaat masala and the remaining lemon juice. Serve hot, accompanied by a green salad and Mint chutney (page 10).

◀ *Cottage Cheese Tikka*

Tandoori Cottage Cheese Salad

Serves: 4-5　　　　　Preparation time: 2 hours　　　　　Cooking time: 15 minutes

Ingredients:

Cottage cheese (*paneer*) .... *1 kg*	Salt to taste
Capsicum .... *20 gms*	Cream .... *100 ml / ½ cup*
Tomatoes .... *20 gms*	Yoghurt, drained .... *150 gms / ¾ cup*
Onions .... *20 gms*	Gramflour/Cornflour .... *30 gms / 2 tbs*
Pineapple .... *20 gms*	Red chilli powder .... *10 gms / 2 tsp*
Black cumin (*shah jeera*) .... *3 gms / ½ tsp*	Saffron (*kesar*) .... *3 gms / ½ tsp*
White pepper powder .... *5 gms / 1 tsp*	Ginger paste (page 10) .... *15 gms / 1 tbs*
Garam masala (page 10) .... *10 gms / 2 tsp*	Garlic paste (page 10) .... *15 gms / 1 tbs*
Turmeric(*haldi*) powder .... *5 gms / 1 tsp*	Butter for basting
Lemon juice .... *15 ml / 1 tbs*	Chaat masala (optional) .... *10 gms / 2 tsp*

Method:

* For recipe of *paneer,* turn to page 10.

1. Wash and cut the cottage cheese, vegetables and pineapple into 4 cm cubes.

2. Mix black cumin, white pepper, garam masala, turmeric powder, 2/3 of the lemon juice and salt together. Add the cottage cheese cubes to this mixture and refrigerate for 1 hour.

3. Mix together, the cream, yoghurt and gramflour/cornflour. Add remaining ingredients (except butter) and whisk to a fine batter.

4. Add the refrigerated cottage cheese cubes, pineapple cubes and vegetables to the batter and leave to marinate for at least 1 hour.

5. Preheat oven to 150-75 °C (300-50 °F).

6. Skewer 6 paneer cubes and 4 vegetables-pineapple pieces per skewer (one portion)and pack tightly together.

7. Roast in an oven/tandoor/charcoal grill for 5-6 minutes, basting regularly with melted butter.

8. Sprinkle chaat masala and the remaining lemon juice. Serve hot, garnished with slices of cucumber, tomato or onion and accompanied by Mint chutney (page 10).

Cottage Cheese Seekh Kabab

Serves: 4-5   Preparation time: 15 minutes   Cooking time: 15 minutes

Ingredients:

Cottage cheese (*paneer*), grated .... *1 kg*
Garam masala (page 10) .... *10 gms / 2 tsp*
Ginger paste (page 10) .... *25 gms / 5 tsp*
Green chillies, chopped *6*
Lemon juice .... *15 ml / 1 tbs*
Onions, grated .... *150 gms / ¾ cup*

Red chilli powder .... *5 gms / 1 tsp*
White pepper powder .... *5 gms / 1 tsp*
Salt to taste
Cornflour .... *15 gms / 3 tsp*
Butter for basting .... *20 gms / 4 tsp*

Method:

     * For recipe of *paneer,* turn to page 10.

1. Mix all the ingredients, adding the cornflour in the end.

2. Divide this mixture into 15 equal portions, shape each portion into a ball.

3. Thread each ball through a skewer. Moisten palm and spread the balls by pressing it along the length of a skewer, into a 8-10 cm long and 1 cm apart kabab.

4. Preheat the oven to 150-75ºC (300-50 ºF)

5. Roast in the oven/tandoor/charcoal grill for 5-6 minutes or until golden brown, basting occasionally with melted butter.

6. Remove from the skewers

7. Serve hot, garnished with slices of cucumber, tomato, onion and accompanied by Mint chutney (page 10).

NOTE: The cottage cheese could be rolled into 8 cm-long kababs and also shallow fried in butter.

STIR FRY

Cottage Cheese Tawa Masala (recipe on following page) ▶

Cottage Cheese Tawa Masala

Serves: 4   Preparation: 10 minutes   Cooking: 15 minutes

Ingredients:

Cottage cheese (*paneer*), cubed .... *450 gms*
Oil + for frying .... *45 ml / 3 tbs*
Cumin (*jeera*) seeds .... *5 gms / 1 tsp*
Onions, chopped .... *150 gms / ¾ cup*
Ginger paste (page 10) .... *25 gms / 5 tsp*
Garlic paste (page 10) .... *25 gms / 5 tsp*
Green chillies, chopped *2*
Coriander powder .... *10 gms / 2 tsp*

Red chilli powder .... *5 gms / 1 tsp*
White pepper powder .... *5 gms / 1 tsp*
Salt to taste
Carom (*ajwain*) seeds .... *1 gm / a pinch*
Tomatoes, chopped .... *150 gms / ¾ cup*
Capsicum, diced .... *120 gms / ½ cup*
Garam masala (page 10) .... *a pinch*
Black cumin (*shah jeera*) ....*2½ gms / ½ tsp*

Method:

    * For recipe of *paneer*, turn to page 10.

1. Heat oil in a *kadhai* (wok) and deep fry the cottage cheese cubes to golden.

2. Heat oil (3 tbs) on a *tawa* (griddle). Add cumin, allow to splutter.

3. Add onions, sauté till golden brown. Add ginger and garlic pastes, green chillies, coriander powder, red chilli powder, white pepper powder, salt and carom seeds. Stir-fry on medium heat. Mix in tomatoes. Cook till the oil separates.

4. Mix in the cottage cheese, capsicum, garam masala and black cumin. Cook for 5 min.

5. Remove to serving platter, top with slit green chillies (optional), serve hot, accompanied by any Indian bread.

Cottage Cheese in a Pickled Curry

Serves: 4-5   Preparation time: 15 minutes   Cooking time: 15 minutes

Ingredients:

Cottage cheese (*paneer*), cubed .... *1 kg*
Olive/Mustard oil .... *110 ml/½ cup*
Cloves (*laung*) *10*
Green cardamoms(*choti elaichi*) *10*
Mustard (*raee*) seeds .... *7 gms / 1½ tsp*
Fenugreek (*methi dana*) seeds *8 gms / 1²/₃ tsp*

Red chillies, whole *16*
Black cumin (*shah jeera*) .... *5 gms / 1 tsp*
Onions, chopped fine .... *200 gms / 1 cup*
Ginger paste (page 10) .... *60 gms / 4 tbs*
Garlic paste (page 10) .... *60 gms / 4 tbs*
Red chilli powder .... *10 gms / 2 tsp*

◀ *Cottage Cheese Tawa Masala*

Turmeric(*haldi*) powder .... *10 gms / 2 tsp*	Sugar .... *10 gms / 2 tsp*
Asafoetida (*heeng*) .... *a pinch*	Garlic cloves, whole 6
Yoghurt, whisked .... *300 gms / 1½ cups*	Lemon juice .... *20 ml / 4 tsp*
Salt to taste	Green coriander, chopped .... *10 gms / 2 tsp*
Black pepper, crushed .... *6 gms / 1¹/₃ tsp*	

Method:

1. Heat oil till it is smoking, lightly stir-fry cloves, cardamoms, mustard seeds, fenugreek seeds, whole red chillies and cumin seeds. Lower the heat.

2. Add onions and brown over medium heat. Stir in ginger-garlic pastes, red chilli powder, turmeric powder and asafoetida, cook for 3-4 minutes. Add yoghurt, bring to a boil, simmer until the oil separates. Add cottage cheese cubes, salt, pepper, sugar, garlic cloves and lemon juice, cook for 2-3 minutes.

3. Serve hot, garnished with green coriander.

Spinach with Cottage Cheese

Serves: 4-5   Preparation time: 25 minutes   Cooking time: 30 minutes

Ingredients:

Spinach (*palak*) leaves ....*1 kg*	Onions, chopped .... *25 gms / 5 tsp*
Cottage cheese (**paneer*)	Tomatoes, finely chopped .... *10 gms / 2 tsp*
cut into cubes ....*250 gms / 1¼ cups*	Ginger, finely chopped .... *25 gms / 5 tsp*
Water .... *2 litres / 10 cups*	Green chillies, chopped 3
Salt to taste	Red chilli powder .... *5 gms / 1 tsp*
Maizeflour (*makke ka atta*) ..... *20 gms / 4 tsp*	Cream .... *10 gms / 2 tsp*
Clarified butter (*ghee*) .... *30 gms / 2 tbs*	

Method:

* For recipe of *paneer,* turn to page 10.

1. Remove stems of the spinach leaves. Wash well and chop finely. Add water and salt, cook for 10 minutes. Allow to cool, drain excess water and blend to a purée.

2. Reheat spinach purée, stir in the maizeflour and cook for 10 minutes.

3. In a separate pan, heat clarified butter, brown the onion, add tomato, ginger, green chillies and red chilli powder. Stir in the spinach purée and cook for 3-5 minutes.

4. Add cottage cheese cubes, cook for another 5 minutes. Stir in the cream.

5. Serve hot, topped with a knob of butter and accompanied by any Indian bread.

Kadhai Paneer

Serves: 4   Preparation time: 15 minutes   Cooking time: 10 minutes

Ingredients:

Cottage cheese (*paneer*),
cut into fingers .... *600 gms*
Oil .... *40 gms / 2²/₃ tbs*
Onions, chopped .... *40 gms / ¼ cup*
Capsicum, julienned .... *40 gms / 2²/₃ tbs*
Red chillies (whole), pounded *15*
Coriander seeds, pounded .... *10 gms / 2 tsp*
Ginger, julienned .... *15 gms / 1 tbs*

Tomato purée .... *150 ml / ¾ cup*
Salt to taste
Fenugreek powder (*kasoori methi*)
.... *5 gms / 1 tsp*
Garam masala (page 10) .... *8 gms / 1²/₃ tsp*
Coriander powder .... *10 gms / 2 tsp*
Black pepper .... *8 gms / 1²/₃ tsp*
Green coriander, chopped .... *15 gms / 1 tbs*

Method:

  * For recipe of *paneer*, turn to page 10

1. Heat oil in a *kadhai* (wok), sauté the onions and capsicum over medium heat for 2 minutes.

2. Add pounded spices and ginger, stir for 1 minute.

3. Mix in the tomato purée and salt, bring to a boil and simmer until the oil separates from the curry.

4. Add cottage cheese and stir gently for 2-3 minutes.

5. Stir in fenugreek powder, garam masala, coriander powder and black pepper.

6. Garnish with chopped coriander leaves and serve hot, accompanied by *Parantha* (page 75), steamed rice and salad.

Mushroom, Capsicum and Cabbage Curry

Serves: 4-5   Preparation time: 10 minutes   Cooking time: 15 minutes

Ingredients:

Mushrooms, quartered .... *600 gms*
Cabbage, shredded .... *120 gms / ½ cup*
Capsicum, julienned .... *60 gms / 4 tbs*
Red chillies, whole *4*
Coriander seeds .... *5 gms / 1 tsp*

Oil .... *120 gms / ½ cup*
Onions, sliced .... *80 gms / ⅓ cup*
Garlic paste (page 10) .... *20 gms / 4 tsp*
Garam masala (page 10) .... *10 gms / 2 tsp*
Salt to taste

| Tomatoes, chopped .... *500 gms / 2½ cups* | Ginger, chopped .... *30 gms / 2 tbs* |
| Green chillies, chopped .... *4* | Green coriander, chopped .... *20 gms / 4 tsp* |

Method:

1. Pound the red chillies and coriander seeds with a pestle. Keep aside.

2. Heat oil (2 tbs) in a *kadhai* (wok). Stir-fry the mushrooms over medium heat for a few minutes. Remove and keep aside.

3. In the same oil, stir-fry the cabbage until the liquid evaporates.

4. Heat the remaining oil in a *kadhai* (wok). Sauté onions till transparent. Add the garlic paste and stir for 20 seconds over medium heat.

5. Add red chillies, coriander, garam masala and salt. Stir for 30 seconds. Add tomatoes and cook till the oil separates from the mixture.

6. Stir in green chillies, ginger and half of the green coriander. Add stir-fried mushrooms and cabbage, cook for a few minutes.

7. Garnish with julienned capsicum and the remaining coriander. Serve hot, accompanied by steamed rice.

Stir-Fried Mushrooms

Serves: 4   Preparation time: 10 minutes   Cooking time: 20 minutes

Ingredients:

Mushrooms .... *½ kg*	Turmeric(*haldi*) powder .... *3 gms / ½ tsp*
Oil .... *22 gms / 4½ tsp*	Garam masala (page 10) .... *3 gms / ½ tsp*
Onions, sliced *2*	Red chilli powder .... *3 gms / ½ tsp*
Garlic paste (page 10) .... *5 gms / 1 tsp*	Salt to taste
Tomato, chopped *1*	Green coriander, chopped .... *15 gms / 1 tbs*

Method:

1. Cut mushrooms in slices.

2. Heat oil and fry onions until golden in colour. Add garlic paste and tomatoes, mix well.

3. Mix in turmeric, garam masala, chilli powder, salt and fry for 3-4 minutes. Stir in mushrooms and simmer until mushrooms are tender, adding very little water if necessary.

4. Garnish with chopped coriander and serve hot.

Tangy Aubergine with Coconut

Serves: 4   Preparation: 20 minutes   Cooking: 30 minutes

Ingredients:

Aubergine / Brinjals (*baigan*) .... *400 gms*
Coriander seeds .... *5 gms / 1 tsp*
Cumin (*jeera*) seeds .... *10 gms / 2 tsp*
Poppy (*khus khus*) seeds .... *5 gms / 1 tsp*
Sesame (*til*) seeds .... *10 gms / 2 tsp*
Tamarind (*imlee*) .... *15 gms / 1 tbs*
Mustard oil (*sarson ka tel*) ......*120 ml / ½ cup*

Ginger paste (page 10) .... *10 gms / 2 tsp*
Garlic paste (page 10) .... *10 gms / 2 tsp*
Turmeric(*haldi*) powder .... *5 gms / 1 tsp*
Red chilli powder .... *10 gms / 2 tsp*
Salt to taste
Curry leaves *10*
Coconut, desiccated ....*35 gms / 2¹/₃ tbs*

Method:

1. Roast coriander, cumin, poppy and sesame seeds on a *tawa* (griddle), pound them, and keep aside. Roast coconut and keep aside.

2. Wash and soak tamarind in warm water (200 ml/1 cup) for 10 minutes. Mash well, squeeze to extract juice and strain, discard the pulp.

3. Slice aubergine about three-fourths of the length without separating them at the stem end.

4. Heat oil in a *kadhai* (wok). Stir-fry the aubergine and set aside.

5. In the same oil, brown the ginger and garlic pastes, ground spices, turmeric, red chilli powder, salt, curry leaves and coconut.

6. Stir occasionally. Add a little water if mixture begins to burn.

7. Add the aubergine alongwith water (200 ml/1 cups). Simmer for 10 minutes.

8. Stir in the tamarind juice and simmer till the curry thickens.

9. Serve hot, accompanied by plain boiled rice or any Indian bread.

CURRIES

Tomatoes stuffed with Mushrooms (recipe on following page) ▶

Tomatoes stuffed with Mushrooms

Serves: 4-5   Preparation time: 15 minutes   Cooking time: 1 hour

Ingredients:

Tomatoes (round and firm) 15
Mushrooms, chopped .... *500 gms / 2½ cups*
Oil .... *30 ml / 2 tbs*
Onions, chopped .... *30 gms / 2 tbs*
Garlic, chopped .... *15 gms / 1 tbs*
Tomato pulp, fresh/canned .. *100 gms / ½ cup*
Green chillies, finely chopped ... *5 gms / 1 tsp*
Salt to taste
Garam masala (page 10) .... *10 gms / 2 tsp*
Mint leaves, chopped .... *10 gms / 2 tsp*
Lemon juice .... *10 ml / 2 tsp*
Black cumin powder (*shah jeera*),
roasted .... *2 gms / ½ tsp*

Green coriander, chopped .... *10 gms / 2 tsp*
For the sauce:
Oil .... *25 ml / 5 tsp*
Green cardamom(*choti elaichi*)powder
.... *3 gms / ²/₃ tsp*
Bay leaf (*tej patta*) *1*
Onions, sliced .... *20 gms / 4 tsp*
Garlic .... *10 gms / 2 tsp*
Tomatoes, chopped .... *300 gms / 1½ cups*
Salt to taste
Cream .... *60 ml / 4 tbs*
Mace (*javitri*) powder .... *3 gms / ²/₃ tsp*

Method:

1. Slice the tops of the tomatoes, scoop out the pulp, drain upside down on a paper towel. Keep the tops aside.

2. Heat oil in a pan, sauté the onions, garlic and tomato pulp over medium heat until the moisture completely evaporates and the oil separates from the curry.

3. Stir in green chillies and mushrooms. Cook over high heat for 10-15 minutes till the water dries.

4. Add salt, garam masala, chopped mint leaves, lemon juice, black cumin powder and half of the green coriander. Cool the mixture.

5. Fill each tomato cup with the mushroom mixture and cover with the tomato top. Bake the stuffed tomatoes in a greased baking tray for 15 minutes.

6. **For the sauce,** heat oil in a pan. Sauté the cardamoms, bay leaf, onions, garlic and chopped tomatoes. Then add water (2 cups) and salt, cook for about 30 minutes.

7. Strain the sauce through a fine sieve. Transfer to a saucepan and bring to a slow boil. Add cream and mace powder.

8. Pour the sauce over the baked tomatoes and sprinkle the remaining half of the green coriander before serving.

◀ *Picture on preceding page*

Stuffed Potatoes in a Fenugreek and Spinach Curry

Serves: 4   Preparation time: 45 minutes   Cooking time: 1 hour

Ingredients:

Potatoes (medium, round) .... *1 kg*
Mint leaves .... *45 gms / 3 tbs*
Coriander leaves .... *90 gms / 6 tbs*
Green chillies, chopped *10*
Cumin (*jeera*) seeds ....*2½ gms / ½ tsp*
Dry mango powder (*amchoor*)   *5 gms / 1 tsp*
Raisins... *20 gms / 4 tsp*
Salt to taste
Oil + for frying .... *90 ml / 6 tbs*
Turmeric (*haldi*) powder ....*2½ gms / ½ tsp*

Tomatoes, chopped................. *80 gms / ¹/₃ cup*
Spinach, chopped.......................... *400 gms*
Fenugreek leaves (*methi*),
  chopped.................................... *105 gms / 7 tbs*
Red chilli powder .... *10 gms / 2 tsp*
Yoghurt .... *45 gms / 3 tbs*
Garam masala (page 10)............ *5 gms / 1 tsp*
Coriander powder .... *5 gms / 1 tsp*
Clarified butter (*ghee*)................. *30 ml / 2 tbs*

Method:

1. Peel and scoop out a spoonful from the centres of the potatoes, deep fry the shells till they are crisp and golden brown.

2. Grind mint, coriander leaves, green chillies, cumin seeds, mango powder, raisins and salt with very little water to make a *chutney* (relish) and set aside.

3. Heat oil (6 tbs) in a *kadhai* (wok). Add turmeric powder, tomatoes, spinach and fenugreek leaves. Sauté lightly.

4. Stir in red chilli powder and salt, cook till the curry thickens. Mix in the yoghurt, garam masala, coriander powder and clarified butter.

5. Remove from heat and allow to cool. Blend to a thick purée and reheat.

6. Spoon the prepared *chutney* into the potatoes.

7. Place potatoes in a shallow dish and pour the curry over them.

8. Serve hot, accompanied by Vegetarian Biryani (page 66).

Minced Peas and Potatoes

Serves: 4-6   Preparation time: 10 minutes   Cooking time: 30 minutes

Ingredients:

Peas, minced ....*300 gms / 1½ cup*
Potatoes (small), diced *5-6*
Green chillies, chopped *1-2*
Ginger, peeled and chopped........... *1½" piece*
Tomatoes, chopped .... *400 gms /2 cups*
Clarified butter (*ghee*) ....*100 ml / ½ cup*
Cumin (*jeera*) seeds .... *5 gms / 1½ tsp*
Cloves (*laung*), ground *6*
Cinnamon (*daalchini*)sticks (1"), ground *2*
Peppercorns, ground *6-8*
Coriander powder .... *15 gms / 1 tbs*
Turmeric (*haldi*) powder .... *5 gms / 1 tsp*
Red chilli powder ....*2½ gms / ½ tsp*
Salt to taste
Coriander, fresh .... *30 gms / 2 tbs*
Garam masala (page 10) .... *15 gms / 1 tbs*

Method:

1. Blend the green chillies, ginger and tomatoes to a purée. Set aside.
2. Heat clarified butter (60 ml / 4 tbs) in a *kadhai* (wok) and brown the minced peas till the oil separates. Set aside.
3. Heat clarified butter (1 tbs), add the cumin seeds, fry for a few seconds. Add the browned peas paste, cloves, cinnamon, peppercorns, ground coriander, turmeric powder, red chilli powder and cook for a few minutes.
4. Stir in the green chillies, ginger and tomato purée, bring to a boil.
5. Mix in the diced potatoes and cook till potatoes become tender.
6. Season with salt and garam masala, garnish with chopped coriander and serve hot.

Hyderabadi Chilli Curry

Serves: 4-5   Preparation time: 15 minutes   Cooking time: 35 minutes

Ingredients:

Green chillies (large),slit lengthwise and deseeded.................................. *200 gms / 1cup*
Tamarind (*imli*) .... *60 gms / 4 tbs*
Coconut, desiccated ....*50 gms / ¼ cup*
Peanuts ....*50 gms / ¼ cup*
Sesame (*til*) seeds ....*50 gms / 3⅔ tbs*
Coriander seeds, roasted .... *20 gms / 4 tsp*
Cumin (*jeera*) powder .... *20 gms / 4 tsp*
Red chilli powder .... *12 gms / 2½ tsp*
Turmeric(*haldi*) powder .... *5 gms / 1 tsp*
Salt to taste
Onion paste, browned (page 10) ....*1 kg*
Ginger paste (page10) .... *15 gms / 1 tbs*
Garlic paste (page10) .... *15 gms / 1 tbs*
Oil ....*500 ml / 2½ cups*
Mustard (*raee*) seed .... *3 gms /⅔ tsp*

Onion (*kalonji*) seed .... *3 gms /²/₃ tsp*   Cumin (*jeera*) seeds .... *3 gms /²/₃ tsp*
Curry leaves *20*

Method:

1. Soak tamarind in warm water for 10 minutes, squeeze out water, retain the pulp.
2. Broil the coconut, peanuts and sesame seeds. Grind to a fine paste. Mix in coriander seeds, cumin powder, red chilli powder, turmeric, salt, browned onion paste and ginger and garlic pastes.
3. Fill this prepared paste into the slit green chillies. Keep aside.
4. Heat oil in a *kadhai* (wok), fry the green chillies to golden brown. Drain excess oil and keep aside.
5. In the same oil, sauté the mustard seed, onion seed, curry leaves and cumin. Stir in left over ground paste and tamarind pulp, cook on low heat for 10 minutes.
6. Add the fried green chillies, simmer for another 10 minutes and serve hot.

Lotus Stems in an Exotic Curry

Serves:4   Preparation time:10 minutes   Cooking time: 30 minutes

Ingredients:

Lotus stem (*kamal kakri*) .... *800 gms*   Salt .... *5 gms / 1 tsp*
Mustard oil ....*250 gms / 1¼ cups*   Cumin (*jeera*)powder ....*2 gms / ¹/₃ tsp*
Water   Cinnamon (*daalchini*) powder *2 gms / ¹/₃ tsp*
Cloves (*laung*) ....*2*   Black cardamom (*bari elaichi*)
Green cardamoms(*choti elaichi*) ....*2*   powder .... *6 gms / 1 tsp*
Fennel (*saunf*) powder .... *30 gms / 2 tbs*   Yoghurt, whisked .... *1-500 kg / 7½ cups*

Method:

1. Scrape away the skin of the lotus stems. Cut into 1½" long pieces, discarding the ends. Wash well and drain.
2. Heat the mustard oil in a *kadhai* (wok) and deep fry the lotus stems till they are half cooked. Drain and keep aside.
3. To the same *kadhai* (wok), add water and the lotus stems, bring to a boil, add all the spices, mix in the yoghurt. Cook till the curry thickens and the lotus stems are tender, stirring regularly.
4. Remove into a serving dish and serve hot.

◀ *Lotus Stems in an Exotic Curry*

Dum Aloo Bhojpuri

Serves: 4-5   Preparation time: 20 minutes   Cooking time: 20 minutes

Ingredients:

Potatoes, small and round .... *600 gms*
Clarified butter (*ghee*) .... *15 gms / 1 tbs*
Onions, grated .... *80 gms / 5¹/₃ tbs*
Ginger paste (page10) .... *30 gms / 2 tbs*
Garlic paste (page10) .... *30 gms / 2 tbs*

For the filling:

Potatoes, boiled and grated .... *200 gms*
Red chilli powder .... *10 gms / 2 tsp*
Turmeric(*haldi*) powder .... *5 gms / 1 tsp*
Garam masala (page 10) .... *10 gms / 2 tsp*

Lemon juice .... *15 ml / 1 tbs*
Salt to taste

For the curry:

Oil .... *50 ml / 3¹/₃ tbs*
Bay leaf (*tej patta*) *1*
Cinnamon (*daalchini*) sticks *2*
Cloves (*laung*) *6*
Green cardamoms (*choti elaichi*) *6*
Black cumin (*shah jeera*) ....*3 gms / ²/₃ tsp*
Yoghurt, whisked .... *150 gms / ¾ cup*

Method:

1. Heat the clarified butter in a pan, add half each of the grated onion, ginger and garlic pastes and fry for 4-5 minutes. Add grated potatoes, red chilli powder, turmeric powder and garam masala. Season with lemon juice and salt. Keep aside.

2. Boil and peel the small potatoes. Scoop out centres and deep fry shells till slightly crisp.

3. Fill each potato shell with the prepared potato mixture. Cover and keep aside.

4. Heat oil in a pan over medium heat. Add bay leaf, cinnamon sticks, cloves, green cardamoms, black cumin seed and fry until they begin to crackle.

5. Mix in the remaining onions, ginger and garlic pastes, stir fry for 2-3 minutes.

6. Add turmeric powder and red chilli powder, stir fry over medium heat for 5-6 minutes. Stir in yoghurt. Cook till the liquids evaporate, stirring regularly. Sprinkle garam masala and season with salt.

7. Arrange the stuffed potatoes in the pan. Sprinkle lemon juice, cover and cook for 3-4 minutes on very low heat.

8. Serve hot, garnished with julienned ginger and accompanied by rice or *Masala pooris*

◀ *Dum Alu Bhojpuri*

Gramflour Dumplings in a Tangy Yoghurt Curry

Serves: 4   Preparation: 45 minutes   Cooking: 30 minutes

Ingredients:

Gramflour (*besan*) .... *120 gms / ½ cup*
Yoghurt .... *360 gms / 1¾ cups*
Salt to taste
Red chilli powder .... *5 gms / 1 tsp*
Turmeric(*haldi*) powder .... *5 gms / 1 tsp*
Soda bi-carbonate .... *a pinch*
Carom (*ajwain*) seeds .... *2.5 gms / ½ tsp*
Green chillies, chopped *5*

Groundnut oil + for frying .... *60 ml / 4 tbs*
Potatoes, cut into rounds .... *150 gms*
Onion, cut in ¼" thick rounds .... *150 gms*
Cumin (*jeera*) seeds .... *2.5 gms / ½ tsp*
Mustard (*raee*) seeds .... *1.25 gms / ¼ tsp*
Fenugreek (*methi dana*) seeds
.... *1.25 gms / ¼ tsp*
Red chillies, whole *4*

Method:

1. Whisk yoghurt, salt, red chilli powder, turmeric and half the gramflour together in a bowl. Keep aside.

2. Sieve the other half of gramflour and soda bi-carbonate together, add the carom seeds and enough water to make a thick batter. Beat well.

3. Add green chillies.

4. Heat enough oil in a *kadhai* (wok) to deep fry.

5. Drop large spoonfuls of the batter in the oil to get 1½" puffy dumplings.

6. Fry till golden brown on all sides. Remove and keep aside.

7. Heat oil (45 ml/3 tbs) in a *handi* (pot), add the yoghurt mixture and water (720 ml/ 3 cups). Bring to a boil, reduce and simmer for 8-10 minutes, stirring constantly to avoid the yoghurt from curdling.

8. Add potatoes and onions, cook till potatoes are tender.

9. Add dumplings, simmer for 35 minutes, remove from heat and transfer to a serving bowl.

10. Heat the remaining oil (15 ml/1 tbs) in a small pan. Add the cumin, mustard and fenugreek seeds, sauté till they crackle. Add whole red chillies, remove from fire and pour this tempering over the hot curry.

11. Serve hot, garnished with chopped coriander and accompanied by boiled rice.

Shahi Paneer

Serves: 4-5   Preparation time: 30 minutes   Cooking time: 20 minutes

Ingredients:

Cottage cheese (*paneer*), fingers .... *1 kg*
Oil ....*80 ml / 5¹/₃ tbs*
Cloves (*laung*) *6*
Bay leaves (*tej patta*) *2*
Cinnamon (*daalchini*)sticks........................*3*
Green cardamoms(*choti elaichi*) *6*
Onions paste (page 10) ....*200 gms / 1 cup*
Ginger paste (page 10) ....*40 gms / 2²/₃ tbs*
Garlic paste (page 10) ....*40 gms / 2²/₃ tbs*
Red chilli powder ....*10 gms / 2 tsp*
Turmeric(*haldi*) powder ....*4 gms / ³/₄ tsp*
Coriander powder ....*5 gms / 1 tsp*

Cashewnut paste ....*10 gms / 2 tsp*
Salt to taste
Red colouring ....*¹/₃ tsp*
Yoghurt, whisked ....*180 gms / ³/₄ cup*
Sugar ....*10 gms / 2 tsp*
Cream ....*120 ml / ²/₃ cup*
Garam masala (page 10) ....*8 gms / 1²/₃ tsp*
Green cardamom(*choti elaichi*) powder
....*3 gms / ²/₃ tsp*
Mace (*javitri*) powder ....*3 gms / ²/₃ tsp*
Vetivier (*kewda*) ....*3 drops*
Saffron (*kesar*)(dissolved in 1 tbs milk) *½ gm*

Method:

* For recipe of *paneer,* turn to page 10.

1. Heat oil in a pan, add cloves, bay leaves, cinnamon sticks and green cardamoms, sauté over medium heat until they begin to crackle. Add the onion paste and stir-fry for 2-3 minutes.

2. Stir in the ginger and garlic pastes, red chilli powder, turmeric powder, coriander powder, cashewnut paste, salt and colour.

3. Add yoghurt, warm water (½ cup) and sugar, bring to a slow boil and then simmer until the oil separates.

4. Allow the curry to cool, remove whole spices and blend to a smooth consistency.

5. Reheat the curry, stir in the cream, garam masala, cardamom powder, mace powder, vetivier and saffron mixture.

6. Add the cottage cheese fingers, cook further for 5 minutes.

7. Serve hot, garnished with chopped coriander, accompanied by any dry vegetable preparation and *Paranthas* (page 75).

Potato and Paneer Dumplings in Curry

Serves: 6   Preparation time: 30 minutes   Cooking time: 1 hour

Ingredients:

For the dumplings:
Potatoes, boiled and mashed 3-4
Cottage cheese (*paneer*), grated ... *500 gms*
Green coriander, chopped .... *45 gms / 3 tbs*
Mixed nuts, finely chopped ...... *45 gms / 3 tbs*
Turmeric(*haldi*) powder .... *2 gms / ½ tsp*
Asafoetida (*heeng*) powder .... *a pinch*
Ginger, finely shredded .... *15 gms / 1 tbs*
Green chillies,deseeded ,finely chopped *1-2*
Dry mango powder (*amchoor*)   *2 gms / ½ tsp*
Lemon juice .... *5 ml / 1 tsp*
Salt .... *7 gms / 1½ tsp*
Cornflour .... *30 gms / 2 tbs*
Oil for frying

For the curry:
Cashewnuts/almonds
finely chopped .... *40 gms / 2²/₃ tbs*
Ginger, finely chopped .... *15 gms / 1 tbs*
Green chillies, chopped *2*
Coriander powder .... *7 gms / 1½ tsp*
Cumin (*jeera*), ground .... *5 gms / 1 tsp*
Turmeric(*haldi*) powder .... *2 gms / ½ tsp*
Water ....*250 ml / 1¼ cups*
Clarified butter (*ghee*) .... *75 ml / 5 tbs*
Cumin (*jeera*) seeds .... *5 gms / 1 tsp*
Cinnamon(*daalchini*) stick (1" piece) *1*
Cloves (*laung*) *4*
Tomatoes, finely chopped ... *600 gms / 3 cups*
Salt to taste

Method:

     * For recipe of *paneer,* turn to page 10.

1. Knead the grated cottage cheese till it is of a smooth and creamy texture. Add the mashed potatoes, coriander, mixed nuts, turmeric powder, asafoetida powder, ginger, green chillies, dry mango powder, lemon juice, salt and cornflour, knead until the ingredients are thoroughly mixed in.

2. Lightly oil your hands and divide the mixture into 12 portions. Roll each portion into a ball. Place all the balls on a tray lined with plastic wrap and set aside.

3. Heat oil in a *kadhai* (wok) to 175 °C (350 °F). Slide in a few balls at a time and fry until golden brown on all sides.

4. Remove, drain excess oil on paper towel and keep aside.

5. **For the curry**, process together the nuts, ginger, green chillies, ground coriander, ground cumin, turmeric powder and enough water to make a smooth paste. Set aside.

6. Moderately heat, the clarified butter in a heavy bottomed pan, stir-fry the cumin seeds, cinnamon stick and cloves for 10-15 seconds.

7. Stir in half of the tomatoes and the prepared paste, cook until the liquid from the tomatoes dries off and the oil separates.

8. Add the remaining tomatoes, water and salt. Cover the pan and simmer for 10-15 minutes or until the curry has thickened slightly.

9. Carefully slip in the dumplings and bring the curry to a boil.

10. Spoon out the dumplings into a serving dish, pour the curry on top and garnish with fresh coriander and cream.

11. Serve hot, accompanied by any Indian bread and green salad.

Baby Corn Sabzi

Serves: 4   Preparation time: 10-15 minutes   Cooking time: 20 minutes

Ingredients:

Baby corn (fresh or canned) .... *1½ kg*	Tomato puree .... *200 gms / 1 cup*
Ginger-garlic paste (page 10) ... *20 gms / 4 tsp*	Yoghurt, whisked .... *200 gms / 1 cup*
Oil .... *15 ml / 1 tbs*	Green peas (shelled) .... *100 gms / ½ cup*
Cumin (*jeera*) seeds .... *3 gms / ½ tsp*	Salt .... *10 gms / 2 tsp*

Method:

1. Prepare ginger and garlic paste. Obtain extract by squeezing out the liquid from the paste, retain the liquid and discard the pulp.

2. Peel and boil the baby corn. Dice into half inch cubes. In case of canned, just dice into cubes.

3. Heat oil in *kadhai* (wok), add cumin seeds and sauté till they start to crackle.

4. Stir in tomato puree, cook till the raw flavour diminishes, for about 6-8 minutes.

5. Stir in the yoghurt, baby corn and green peas, let it cook for about 5 minutes.

6. Season with salt and the ginger-garlic paste extract. Cook for another 2 minutes or until the curry thickens.

7. Serve hot, garnished with chopped coriander and accompanied by any Indian bread.

ACCOMPANIMENTS & DESSERTS

Lemon Rice (recipe on following page) ▶

Lemon Rice

Serves: 4   Preparation time: 5 minutes   Cooking time: 25-35 minutes

Ingredients:

Rice, basmati or any
long grain variety .... *100 gms / ½ cup*
Lemon juice .... *80 ml / ⅓ cup*
Water .... *400-480 ml / 2-2⅔ cups*
Salt .... *5 gms / 1 tsp*
Oil / Clarified butter (ghee).......... *45 ml / 3 tbs*
Cashewnuts, chopped .... *75 gms / ½ cup*

Lentils (*Urad daal*), split .... *7 gms / ½ tbs*
Mustard (*raee*) seeds .... *5 gms / 1 tsp*
Red chillies, whole *2-3*
Turmeric(*haldi*) powder .... *½ gm / ⅓ tsp*
Coriander, coarsely chopped ... *45 gms / 3 tbs*
Coconut, fresh, shredded .... *25 gms / ¼ cup*

Method:

1. Wash and soak the rice in water for 10 minutes. Drain and keep aside.

2. Boil water in a heavy pan. Stir in rice, salt and oil (7 ml / ½ tbs). Cover tightly, reduce heat
   and simmer without stirring until rice is fluffy and tender and water is fully
   absorbed. Set aside.

3. Heat remaining oil in a small pan, stir-fry the cashewnuts until golden brown. Drain
   excess oil and spoon cashewnuts over the cooked rice. Replace cover.

4. Raise the heat slightly, sauté the lentils and mustard seeds till the lentils turn reddish
   brown, mustard seeds splutter and add whole red chillies and remove from heat.

5. Gently fold in the lentils, turmeric, lime juice, coriander and coconut into the cooked rice
   until well mixed.

6. Serve hot, accompanied by natural yoghurt.

Vegetable Biryani

Serves: 4-5   Preparation time: 45 minutes   Cooking time: 30 minutes

Ingredients:

Rice, basmati or any long
grain variety .... *200 gms / 1 cup*
Carrots, diced and parboiled ... *20 gms / 4 tsp*
Cauliflower, small pieces .... *20 gms / 4 tsp*
Green peas, parboiled .... *20 gms / 4 tsp*
Mushrooms, quartered .... *20 gms / 4 tsp*

Oil .... *60 ml / 4 tbs*
Cloves (*laung*) *4*
Cinnamon (*daalchini*) stick, medium *1*
Bay leaf (*tej patta*) *1*
Green cardamom(*choti elaichi*) *3*
Black cumin (*shah jeera*) .... *5 gms / 1 tsp*

◀ *Lemon Rice (picture on preceding page)*

Onions, chopped .... *50 gms / ¼ cup*	Onions, sliced and fried .... *10 gms / 1 onion*
Ginger paste (page 10) .... *10 gms / 2 tsp*	Mace (*javitri*) powder .... *2 gms / ½ tsp*
Red chilli powder .... *3 gms / ²/₃ tsp*	Lemon juice .... *15 ml / 1 tbs*
White pepper powder .... *2 gms / ½ tsp*	Ginger, julienned .... *3 gms / ²/₃ tsp*
Salt to taste	Cashewnuts, fried golden *10*
Water .... *500 ml / 2½ cups*	Coriander, chopped .... *5 gms / 1 tsp*
For garnishing:	Cream .... *30 ml / 2 tbs*
Green chillies, slit .... *5 gms / 1 tsp*	

Method:

1. Clean, wash and soak the rice for 30 minutes.
2. Heat oil in a heavy bottomed pan, sauté the cloves, cinnamon stick, bay leaf, cardamom and black cumin seeds until they begin to crackle.
3. Add onions, stir-fry till transparent. Stir in ginger paste and red chilli powder, all vegetables alongwith white pepper and salt. Cook for 3-4 minutes.
4. Stir in the drained rice and water, bring to a boil, lower heat, cover and cook till the rice is almost done.
5. Remove the lid, sprinkle slit green chillies, fried onions, mace powder, lemon juice, julienned ginger, cashewnut, green coriander and cream.
6. Seal lid with dough, cook on very low heat for 10-15 minutes.
7. Serve hot, accompanied by natural yoghurt.

Peas Pulao

Serves: 4-5   Preparation time: 5 minutes   Cooking time: 30 minutes

Ingredients:

Rice, basmati .... *400 gms / 2 cups*	Cumin (*jeera*) seeds .... *10 gms / 2 tsp*
Fresh peas, boiled .... *200 gms / 1 cup*	Salt to taste
Oil .... *10 ml / 2 tsp*	Water

Method:

1. Clean, wash and soak the rice for 10 minutes.
2. Heat oil in a heavy bottomed pot, sauté the cumin seeds till they crackle.
3. Add the boiled peas and salt. Stir-fry for a few minutes and set aside.
4. Put water to boil in a big pot, cook the rice, drain excess water.
5. Gently fold the peas into the rice and serve hot, accompanied by any curry dish.

Broccoli and Carrot Pulao

Serves: 4-5   Preparation time: 5 minutes   Cooking time: 30 minutes

Ingredients:

Rice, basmati .... *400 gms /2 cups*
Broccoli, (small flowerets) .... *150 gms /³⁄₄ cup*
Carrots, diced, parboiled ...... *100 gms /¹⁄₂cup*
Oil .... *30 ml / 2 tbs*
Cumin (*jeera*) seeds .... *8 gms / 1¹⁄₂ tsp*

Bay leaf (*tej patta*) *1*
Cloves (*laung*) *3*
Black peppercorns .... *5 gms / 1 tsp*
Salt to taste
Water .... *1 litre / 6 cups*

Method:

1. Clean, wash and soak the rice in water for 10 minutes. Drain and keep aside.

2. Heat oil in a heavy bottomed pan, sauté cumin seeds, bay leaf, cloves, and black peppercorns till they crackle. Add the carrots, broccoli and salt, stir-fry for 3-4 min.

3. Remove and discard whole spices, set the vegetables aside.

4. Boil water in a separate pot, cook the rice until done and drain excess water.

5. Gently fold in the cooked vegetables into the rice, transfer to a serving platter. Serve hot, accompanied by any curry dish.

Daal Sultani

Serves: 4-5   Preparation time: 40 minutes   Cooking time: 30 minutes

Ingredients:

Pigeon peas (*toovar daal*) *250 gms / 1¹⁄₄ cups*
Turmeric(*haldi*) powder .... *5 gms / 1 tsp*
Salt to taste
Butter .... *50 gms / ¹⁄₄ cup*
Onions, quartered .... *150 gms / ³⁄₄ cup*

Black cumin (*shah jeera*) .... *5 gms / 1 tsp*
Red chilli powder .... *10 gms / 2 tsp*
Cream .... *30 ml / 2 tbs*
Saffron, (*kesar*) soaked in cream .... *1 gm*

Method:

1. Wash and soak the lentils for 30 minutes. Drain and boil in water (2 litres), removing the scum that collects on top.

2. Reduce heat. Add turmeric (2/3 tsp), salt, cover and cook until the lentils are soft.

3. Heat butter in a separate pan, sauté onions, cumin seeds, turmeric (1/3 tsp) and red chilli powder till the seeds crackle. Add cooked lentils, cover and cook for 2 minutes.

4. Pour the cream-saffron mixture over the lentils, serve hot, accompanied by boiled rice.

Daal Makhani

Serves: 4 　　　　Preparation time: 6-7 hours 　　　　Cooking time: 3 hours

Ingredients:

Black lentils, whole
(*black urad daal*) .... *300 gms / 1½ cups*
Butter .... *120 gms / ½ cup*
Ginger paste (page 10) .... *20 gms / 4 tsp*
Garlic paste (page 10) .... *20 gms / 4 tsp*
Green chillies, sliced *2*

Tomato purée .... *160 ml / ²/₃ cup*
Salt to taste
Chilli powder .... *5 gms / 1 tsp*
Green coriander, chopped .... *10 gms / 2 tsp*
Cream .... *160 ml / ²/₃ cup*

Method:

1. Soak lentils for at least 3 hrs; best soaked overnight.

2. Cook lentils in water(1½ lts) over low heat till grain splits. Stir to mash them. Set aside.

3. Heat butter, fry ginger and garlic pastes. Add green chillies, tomato puree, salt and chilli powder. Cook for 2-3 minutes, add the cooked lentils alongwith coriander and cream (leaving 1 tbs aside). Cook further for 10-15 minutes, stirring occasionally.

4. Serve hot, garnished with the reserved cream and accompanied by any Indian bread.

Rasam

Serves:4 　　　　Preparation: 30 minutes 　　　　Cooking: 15 minutes

Ingredients:

Lentils(*toovar daal*), washed *100 gms / ½ cup*
Oil .... *15 ml / 1 tbs*
Mustard (*raee*) seeds .... *4 gms / 1 tsp*
Red chillies, whole *5*
Curry leaves *10*
Asafoetida (*heeng*) .... *1 gm*

Garlic, crushed.......................... *30 gms / 2 tbs*
Turmeric (*haldi*) powder .... *a pinch*
Tomatoes, quartered *2-3*
Peppercorns .... *3 gms / 3-4*
Green chilli, deseeded and slit *1*
Tamarind (*imli*) pulp .... *100 gms / ½ cup*

Method:

1. Heat oil in a pan. Sauté mustard seeds till they crackle. Add whole red chillies, curry leaves, asafoetida and garlic, stir for a few seconds. Add turmeric, lentils, tomatoes, peppercorns, green chilli, tamarind pulp and salt to taste. Stir in 1 litre of water.

2. Bring to a boil and let it simmer until the lentils are mashed.

3. Serve hot as a starter or as an accompaniment to a meal.

◀ *Daal Makhani*

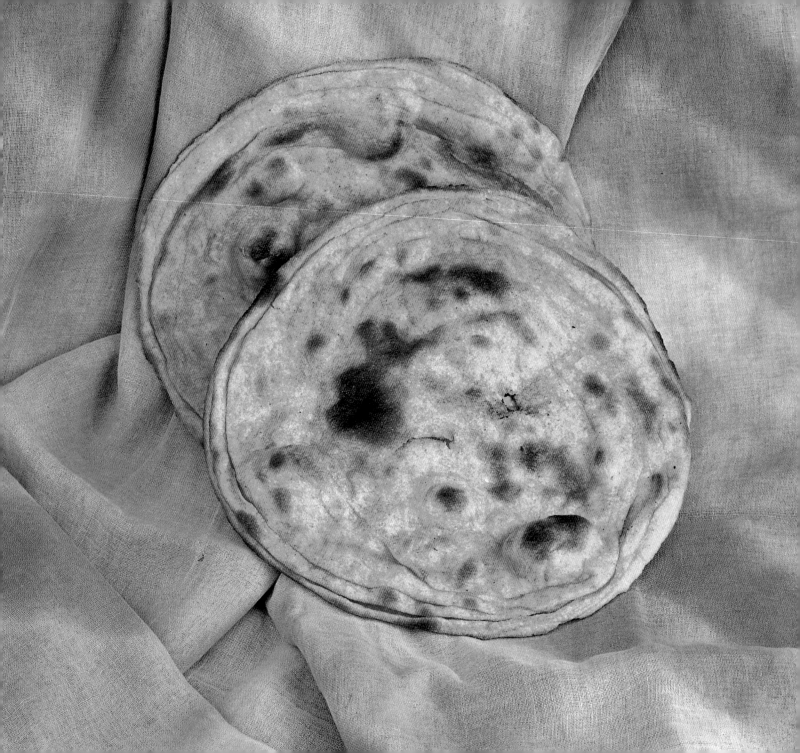

Naan

Serves: 4-5   Preparation time: 3 hours   Cooking time: 20 minutes

Ingredients:

Flour, sieved .... *500 gms / 2½ cups*	Sugar .... *10 gms / 2 tsp*
Salt to taste	Milk ....*50 ml / 3²/₃ tbs*
Baking soda................................. *1 gm / ¼ tsp*	Clarified butter (*ghee*)/Oil......... *25 gms / 5 tsp*
Baking powder......................... *5 gms / 1 tsp*	Onion (*kalonji*) seeds .... *3 gms /²/₃ tsp*
Egg, whisked *1*	Melon (*magaz*) seeds .... *5 gms / 1 tsp*

Method:

1. Mix flour, salt, baking soda, baking powder, egg, sugar and milk. Add enough water to knead into a soft and smooth dough. Cover with a moist cloth, keep aside for 10 minutes.

2. Add oil, knead and punch the dough, cover and keep aside to ferment for 2 hours.

3. Divide the dough into 6 balls, place on a lightly floured surface, sprinkle onion and melon seeds, flatten the balls slightly, cover and keep aside for 5 minutes.

4. Flatten each ball to make a round disc, stretch on one side to form an elongated oval. Place on a greased baking tray. Bake in a preheated oven (175 °C / 350 °F) for 2-3 min.

5. Serve hot as an accompaniment to any curry dish.

Chappatis

Serves: 4-6   Preparation time: ½ hour   Cooking time: ½ hour

Ingredients:

Whole wheat flour, sieved... *225 gms / 2 cups*	Water ....*150 ml / ¾ cup*
Salt (optional) .... *3 gms / ½ tsp*	Clarified butter (*ghee*)............... *15 gms / 1 tbs*

Method:

1. Mix flour and salt in a bowl. Add water, knead into a smooth and elastic dough. Cover and keep aside for 20 mins at room temperature.

2. Place the dough on a floured board. Divide into 8 portions, roll out each into a thin round, the size of a snack plate.

3. Heat a *tawa* (griddle). Place one round on the griddle. Cook until tiny spots appear on one side, flip over and cook the other side for a few seconds. Flip over again and roast till it is of pale golden colour on both sides.

4. Brush lightly with butter and serve hot as an accompaniment to any curry dish.

Masala Poori

Serves: 16   Preparation time: 15 minutes+½ hour-3 hours   Cooking time: ½ hour
(for dough resting)

Ingredients:

Flour, sieved .... *400 gms / 2 cups*
Salt .... *2 gms / ½ tsp*
Cayenne pepper or paprika .... *a pinch*
Turmeric(*haldi*) powder .... *a pinch*
Coriander powder .... *10 gms / 2 tsp*

Cumin (*jeera*) ground .... *7 gms / 1²/₃ tsp*
Oil or Butter, melted .... *30 gms /2 tbs*
Water, warm .... *160 ml / ¾ cup*
Oil for frying

Method:

1. Mix the flour, salt, cayenne pepper, turmeric, coriander and cumin. Add oil/butter and rub it in till it is thoroughly incorporated. Add water, knead into a medium soft dough.

2. Lightly oil your palms and knead until the dough is silky smooth and pliable. Shape into a smooth ball. Brush with oil and keep aside for 3 hours.

3. Knead again briefly, divide into 16 equal portions and shape into balls.

4. Compress each into a 2" patty. Dip one end of the patty in oil and roll out into a 5" round, place on a flat surface. Similarly, roll out the other portions.

5. Heat oil in a *kadhai* (wok). Carefully slip one round into the hot oil. Fry until it puffs up and is golden brown on both sides. Remove and drain on paper towels.

6. Serve hot as an accompaniment to any curry dish.

Cauliflower Stuffed Parantha

Serves: 4-5   Preparation time: 45 minutes   Cooking time: 15 minutes

Ingredients:

Whole wheat flour, sieved .... *800 gms /4 cups*
Salt .... *8 gms / ½ tsp*
Clarified butter (*ghee*) .... *245 ml / 1¼ cup*
Water, warm .... *280 ml / 1¹/₃ cups*

For the filling:

Ginger, grated .... *30 gms / 2 tbs*
Cauliflower, grated .... *450 gms / 2¾ cups*
Garam masala (page 10) .... *10 gms / 2 tsp*

Method:

1. Mix flour and salt in a bowl. Incorporate clarified butter (1/3 cup). Add water gradually and knead to a smooth dough. Divide into 20 equal portions and shape into balls. Cover with a damp cloth and keep aside for 10 minutes.

2. Heat clarified butter in a pan over moderate heat, stir-fry the ginger and cauliflower until the cauliflower softens. Stir in garam masala and salt. Remove from heat, divide the filling into 10 portions and allow to cool.

3. Flatten a ball of dough into a 2" patty. Dust both sides with flour, roll out into a 6" round. Similarly roll out other portions.

4. Spread one portion of filling evenly over one round leaving a half inch border around the edges. Place another round on top of the filling. Gently smooth the surface to ease out air bubbles, press around the edges to seal in filling. Cover and set aside on a lightly floured surface. Similarly, prepare the other portions.

5. Heat a *tawa* (griddle), brush the surface with clarified butter. Place the stuffed *parantha* on the griddle and cook for a few seconds, brush with clarified butter, turn over and similarly cook on the other side. Both sides of the *parantha* should be crisp and delicately browned. Remove and serve immediately.

   NOTE: For variation, substitute Cauliflower with mashed **Potatoes** or grated **White Raddish** or mashed **Peas**.

Parantha

Serves: 4-5   Preparation time: 20 minutes   Cooking time: 10 minutes

Ingredients:

Whole wheat flour .... *500 gms / 2½ cups*   Clarified butter *(ghee)*, melted . *200 gms / 1 cup*
Salt to taste   Water .... *250 ml / 1¼ cups*

Method:

1. Sieve the flour and salt in a bowl, incorporate clarified butter (2 tbs), add water gradually and knead to a smooth dough.

2. Divide into 5 equal portions and shape into balls. Dust with flour, cover and keep aside for 10 minutes.

3. Flatten each ball of dough and roll out. Brush with clarified butter and fold over. Brush the folded surface with clarified butter and fold over again to form a triangle. Roll out the triangle with a rolling pin.

4. Heat a *tawa* (griddle) and brush the surface with clarified butter. Place the *parantha* on the *tawa* and cook for a few minutes. Coat with a little clarified butter, turn over and similarly cook on the other side. Both sides of the *parantha* should be crisp and delicately browned.

5. Remove and serve immediately.

◀ *Parantha (Picture on page 72)*

Lavang Latika

Serves: 4   Preparation time: 35 minutes   Cooking time: 30 minutes

Ingredients:

For the dough:

Flour, sieved	*200 gms / 1 cup*
Oil	*30 gms / 2 tbs*
Saffron (soaked in 1 tbs water)	*a few strands*
Water	*60 ml / 4 tbs*

For the filling:

Khoya, mashed (page 10)	*125 gms / ³/₅ cup*
Almonds, slivered	*20 gms / 4 tsp*

Pistachios, slivered	*20 gms / 4 tsp*
Clove, powdered	*3 gms / ¹/₂ tsp*
Sugar, powdered	*30 gms / 2 tbs*
Cloves (*laung*)	*12*
Oil for frying	

For the sugar syrup:

Sugar	*500 gms / 2¹/₂ cups*
Water	*700 gms / 3¹/₂ cups*

Method:

1. Make a well in the centre of the sieved flour.

2. Put the saffron and oil into the well and incorporate into the flour.

3. Add water gradually and knead to make a hard dough. Cover with a wet cloth and allow to rest for 15 minutes.

4. For the stuffing, mix khoya, pistachios, almonds, powdered clove and powdered sugar. Divide into 12 equal portions.

5. For the sugar syrup, boil sugar with water till the sugar is completely dissolved, simmer for 2-3 minutes.

6. Divide the dough into 12 equal portions and shape into balls. Roll out each of these balls into 6" diameter pancakes.

7. Place one portion of filling in centre of each pancake, brush the edges with water.

8. Fold the pancakes from the right edge to centre and press firmly to seal in the filling. Repeat from the left edge, to give a 2" wide strip.

9. Keeping the folded side out, make a ring with the strip. Brush edges with water and press firmly to seal, secure with a clove.

10. Shallow fry on a very low heat for 8-10 minutes till crisp and golden brown in colour. Remove and drain excess oil.

11. Dip in hot sugar syrup to submerge completely, turning gently if required. Allow to soak for 2-3 minutes. Remove and drain excess syrup.

12. Arrange neatly on a serving dish and serve.

◀ *Lavang Latika*

Gajar ka Halwa

Serves: 10-12   Preparation time:10 minutes   Cooking time: 1 hour

Ingredients:

Carrots, washed, peeled, shredded .... *1 kg*
Milk .... *600 ml / 2½ cups*
Sugar .... *110 gms / ½ cup*
Brown sugar .... *85 gms / ½ cup*
Green cardamoms(*choti elaichi*), ground
.... *5 gms / 1 tsp*
Butter/Oil .... *80 ml / ⅓ cup*

Almonds, sliced or slivered ...... *30 gms / 2 tbs*
Raisins .... *40 gms / 2½ tbs*
Walnuts, chopped .... *40 gms / 2½ tbs*
Cloves (*laung*), ground .... *1 gms / ¼ tsp*
Nutmeg (*jaiphal*), ground .... *1 gms / ¼ tsp*
Cinnamon (*daalchini*), ground *1 gms / ¼ tsp*

Method:

1. Combine carrots and milk in a pan, bring to a boil, reduce to moderate heat, cook for 20-25 minutes, stirring continuously, till the mixture is nearly dry.

2. Add white sugar, brown sugar and half of the cardamom, continue stirring. Cook for 10-12 minutes. Remove pan from heat and set aside.

3. Heat oil in a pan over moderate heat, fry almonds until golden. Stir in the carrot mixture alongwith raisins, walnuts and ground spices. Cook till the mixture (*halwa*) begins to separate from the sides. Serve hot, garnished with remaining cardamoms.

Badam ka Halwa

Serves: 4-5   Preparation time: 30 minutes   Cooking time: 20 minutes

Ingredients:

Almonds, blanched,
chopped .... *500 gms / 2½ cups*
Milk .... *200 gms / 1 cup*
Clarified butter (*ghee*) .... *200 gms / 1 cup*

Sugar .... *500 gms / 2½ cups*
Green cardamom (*choti elaichi*)
powder .... *6 gms / 1⅓ tsp*
Saffron (*kesar*) .... *1 gm / ¼ tsp*

Method:

1. Blend the almonds with a little milk to make a fine paste.

2. Heat clarified butter in a pan. Cook almond paste over medium heat until it becomes light golden. Add milk and sugar, cook for 10-15 minutes, until the mixture becomes thick. Remove from heat. Add cardamom powder and saffron.**To serve cold**: spread on a greased tray, cut into small squares. **To serve hot:** ladle individual portion into a dessert plate.

◀ *Gajar ka Halwa*

Mango Kulfi

Serves: 4-6   Preparation time: 20 minutes   Cooking time: 30 minutes
                                    + 8 hrs for setting

Ingredients:

Mango pulp .... *450 ml / 2¼ cups*   Saffron (*kesar*) .... *a few strands*
Milk .... *1 litre / 4¼ cups*   Cream (heavy) .... *150 ml / ¾ cups*
Sugar .... *40 gms / 2²/₃ tbs*

Method:

1. Boil milk into a heavy bottomed pan, lower heat, let it simmer, add sugar, cook till quantity is reduced to a third and it is thick and creamy.
2. Add mango pulp and saffron, cook further for 2 minutes, cool to room temperature and mix in the cream.
3. Spoon the mixture into 6-8 moulds. Cover tightly with foil and freeze for at least 6 hours. Shake the mould thrice during first hour of freezing.
4. Remove from refrigerator, dip the bottom of the mould in hot water and invert onto a dish. Serve immediately.

Badami Kheer

Serves: 4-5   Preparation time: 30 minutes   Cooking time: 30 minutes

Ingredients:

Almonds, blanched , halved ..... *50 gms / ¼ cup*   Lemon rind, grated .... *1 tsp*
Milk, full cream .... *1 litre / 5 cups*   Sugar .... *150 gms / ¾ cup*
Long-grain rice .... *100 gms / ½ cup*   Rose water (*gulab jal*) .... *4-5 drops*
Green cardamom(*choti elaichi*) *6 gms / 1¹/₃ tsp*

Method:

1. Soak the rice in water for 30 minutes. Drain and keep aside.
2. Boil milk over medium heat. Add rice, green cardamoms and lemon rind, cook until the rice is slightly over done.
3. Add the sugar and almonds and cook for 5-10 minutes, stirring from time to time with a wooden spoon. Check the consistency—it should be quite thick and with a slightly golden in colour.
4. Add rose water and garnish with cherries (optional). Serve hot or chilled.

Besan Ladoo

Makes: 2 dozen balls   Preparation time:10 minutes   Cooking time:20 minutes

Ingredients:

Gramflour (*besan*), sifted .... *200 gms / 2 cups*   Walnuts, chopped .... *30 gms / 2 tbs*
Butter(unsalted)/Oil .... *180 ml / ¾ cup*   Nutmeg (*jaiphal*), ground .... *a pinch*
Coconut, dried and grated .... *30 gms / 2 tbs*   Sugar .... *110 gms / ¾ cup*

Method:

1. Melt butter/oil in a heavy bottomed pan over moderately low heat. Add gramflour, coconut, walnuts and nutmeg, cook, for about 5 minutes stirring constantly. Add sugar and continue to cook for 10-15 minutes or until the mixture is thick and deep golden brown.

2. Turn onto a clean flat surface, when cool enough to handle, shape into 24 equal sized balls.

3. Garnish with slivered nuts and serve at room temperature. Can be stored upto 10-15 days.

Coconut Burfee

Serves: 4   Preparation: 10 minutes   Cooking: 10 minutes

Ingredients:

Coconut powder .... *600 gms / 2½ cups*   Saffron (*kesar*) .... *a few strands*
Sugar .... *60 gms / ¼ cup*   Green cardamom(*choti elaichi*) powder
Water .... *80 ml / 1/3 cup*   .... *5 gms / 1 tsp*
Sweet Ittar .... *1 drop*   Pistachios, slivered .... *a few*

Method:

1. Heat sugar and water in a pan, stir continuously till sugar is completely dissolved. Bring to a boil.

2. Stir in coconut powder, sweet ittar, saffron and cardamom powder. Cook on low heat for 2-3 minutes.

3. Remove from fire and spread evenly on a greased baking tray.

4. Cool and cut into 8 pieces. Garnish with slivered pistachios.

◀ *Besan Ladoo*

INDEX

Accompaniments

Broccoli and Carrot Pulao 69
Cauliflower Stuffed Parantha 74
Chappati 73
Daal Makhani 71
Daal Sultani 69
Lemon Rice 66
Masala Poori 74
Naan 73
Parantha 75
Peas Pulao 67
Rasam 71
Vegetable Biryani 66

Curries

Baby Corn Sabzi 64
Dum Aloo Bhojpuri 57
Gramflour Dumplings in a Tangy Yoghurt Curry 59
Hyderabadi Chilli Curry 53
Lotus Stems in an Exotic Curry 55
Mined Peas and Potatoes 53
Potato and Paneer Dumplings in Curry 63
Shahi Paneer 61
Stuffed Potatoes in Fenugreek & Spinach Curry .51
Tomatoes stuffed with Mushrooms 50

Desserts

Badam ka Halwa 79
Badami Kheer 81
Besan Ladoo 83
Coconut Burfee 83
Gajar ka Halwa 79
Lavang Latika 77
Mango Kulfi 81

Snacks & Starters

Aloo Kachori 21
Assorted Fritters 17
Batter coated stuffed Tomatoes 23
Bedvi 12
Cottage Cheese Kathi Kabab 28
Khandvi 12
Khasta Kachori 20
Lentil Curry (*Sambhar*) 25
Lentil Kabab 15
Mattar Kachori 19
Rice Flour Pancakes (*Dosa*) 27
Sesame Seed coated Cheese Kababs 13
Steamed Rice Flour Patty (*Idli*) 25
Tandoori Potatoes 23
Yam Kabab 15

Stir-Fry

Cottage Cheese in a Pickled Curry 42
Cottage Cheese Tawa Masala 42
Kadhai Paneer 45
Mushroom Capsicum Cabbage Curry 45
Spinach with Cottage Cheese 43
Stir-Fried Mushrooms 47
Tangy Aubergines with Coconut 48

Tandoori & Dry

Cauliflower seasoned with Ginger 31
Cottage Cheese Seekh Kabab 40
Cottage Cheese Tikka 37
Crispy Cauliflower 33
Crunchy Okra 30
Stuffed Capsicum 33
Stuffed Courgettes (*Teenda*) 35
Tandoori Cottage Cheese Salad 39